BEYOND ZERO
SUM LEADERSHIP

Gordon Peters

PAGE PUBLISHING, INC.
New York, NY

First originally published by Page Publishing, Inc. 2016

ISBN 978-1-68289-126-1 (pbk)
ISBN 978-1-68289-127-8 (digital)
ISBN 978-1-68289-128-5 (hardcover)

Printed in the United States of America

CONTENTS

Gordon Peters, founder, chairman, and CEO of the Institute for Management Studies, is a graduate of the California State University at San Francisco, School of Education, and has taught computer sciences at Delta College, a part of the California State College system. He spent a few years as head of industrial engineering and standards for a midsized manufacturing firm; then, after serving as senior industrial engineer with Lockheed, he was promoted to head of computer methods for Lockheed Missiles and Space Company. Later, as manager of computer operations at Fairchild Semiconductor, he successfully rebuilt the department. He was then recruited to become head of management systems for a large food-processing company, where he was responsible for designing and implementing all management information and control systems. A NYSE firm acquired the company, and Mr. Peters was made assistant to the president and chairman of the strategic planning committee. Recruited by another Fortune 1000 firm, he reorganized its overall management and administration systems, including the cost-accounting systems, information systems, market planning and sales systems, and production control and distributions systems and was promoted to senior vice president and chief financial officer. Mr. Peters went on to found the Institute for Management Studies (IMS).

From the Author

The institute was founded primarily as a means of bringing together management thought leaders with peers from different organizations to experience not only the finest in professional growth opportunities but also to be able to network among peers from other major organizations and thus learn from and be enriched by both content and context. The decision to found the Institute for Management Studies depended on my ability to "recruit" the top faculty. I therefore first called Dr. Peter Drucker to ask whether, if I were to undertake this effort, he would conduct sessions for me. He agreed, and the institute was born. In the forty years since then, IMS has been fortunate to have such distinguished faculty as Dr. Michael Porter (his first ever management program outside of Harvard), Dr. William Ury (also his first), Dr. Ram Charan, Dr. Kenneth Blanchard, Dr. Stephen Covey, Dr. Peter Senge, Dr. Roosevelt Thomas, Dr. Henry Mintzberg, Dr. C. K. Prahalad, Dr. Peter Schwartz, Dr. Charles Handy, and (literally) hundreds of others conduct IMS sessions for its sponsoring members.

Imagine the experience of spending an entire day, face-to-face, with such leading-edge thinkers as Russell Ackoff, Delorese Ambrose, Chip Bell, Robert Bies, Tony Buzan, Ed Foreman, Vijay Govindarajan, Gordon Hewitt, James Hulbert, Warren McFarlan, Terry Paulson, Judith Segal, Fons Trompenaars, or Albert Vicere, and other world-class faculty. IMS has grown from its original 4 members in San Francisco to over 425 major sponsoring member organizations in twenty-six cities in six countries. IMS is considered the leader in its field and conducts over 350 management seminars each year with over fifteen thousand managers attending.

PREFACE

I have often said that what this county really needs is a good 5¢ cigar and another book on leadership. Not being one to waste my time (or yours), it took me some twenty years to decide that I had something worth writing and, I hope, something worth reading. This book synthesizes fifty-plus years of my journey from teacher, to industrial engineer, to computer systems, to strategic planner, and finally, to CFO of a major company and for the past forty years as founder and chairman of the Institute for Management Studies. Along the way I made some interesting and, I think, useful discoveries (through both experience and experimentation) that are worth sharing. I hope you find some freshness, as my varied experiences put me in touch with all levels, virtually all aspects of all departments, and of a wide variety of businesses and people. However, since this journey has taken some time, many of the examples will seem (and are) a bit dated. I trust you to see through this shortcoming to the principles underlying the approach and to not get bogged down by the specific example I have chosen. But first, let me set the stage.

It was one of those damp, overcast days so typical of San Francisco in December. Nevertheless, this was a very special day for me as I got my first bike last night. So there I was, in the early morning of Christmas day, with my hand-me-down bike from one of my cousins, setting out for a spin around the block. It was a small bike (I was five or six years old at the time) that was made to look like a small motorcycle. I was really excited as I never imagined I would ever get a bike for Christmas, or for that matter anytime, as it was, after all, 1939. I had ridden maybe ten minutes or so in front of my house when the bike and I tangled with a pothole, and down we both went. My cuts and bruises healed quickly, but the bike's injuries were fatal. The pedal shaft was so severely bent that the bike was unusable. My dad was not in a position to pay for the repairs it needed, and so that pothole ended any hope that I might someday compete in the Tour de France.

You see, I was a Depression baby, and times were tough, so tough that some nights we went to bed without dinner. Some nights we had rice soup—an old Swedish recipe handed down by my Swedish American (there, I said it) grandmother. Of course, there were the good days when we had Spam along with some of the things that my mother had canned during the year or a few vegetables we had grown in our backyard. Once in a while, my mother would cook the flowers from the zucchini plants we grew, which was a special treat. On very rare occasions, when my dad was lucky enough to find some work, my brother and I would each get $1 to see a movie *and* have a hamburger at the restaurant next door to the Avenue Theatre in San Francisco. Yes, $1 for both. Of course, we could always save up a little money ourselves by riding to school on the cowcatcher on the back of the San Francisco streetcars instead of using the 5¢ we had been given to ride inside.

These were hard times, but although I knew that others had it better, I never felt that my family had been singled out for some sort of mean-spirited test of character. My parents were, as you might imagine, sometimes under great stress, but we never lacked for affection. They were both very strong people and gave us all they had to give. The most important gift was a value system that has guided me through good and bad times, and I am happy to say my children have inherited that strength of character that my parents gifted to me. The other thing I was blessed with was timing. Being born during the Depression had, I later learned, some advantages. If one had the drive to succeed, was willing to take on responsibility, was open to learning new things and willing to take some risks, there were a lot fewer competitors in the job market.

What has all this got to do with leadership? It has everything to do with it. It is, after all, the value system that you bring to bear on situations that determine the kind of leader you will most likely become and how successful a leader you will be. Is that true all the time? Of course not. There are plenty of ruthless amoral leaders in the world. But by using one's value base as a starting point, it is easier to see how leadership has changed over the years and the problems some of these changes have caused. In chapters 2 and 3 of this book, we will take a brief trip back in history to try to put these changes into a context that may help to understand the impact our values and visions have had on our current (and future) status as a country and as a culture.

A simple example should suffice to illustrate my point. In my early years (high school and college), I did what was necessary to support myself and, later, my family. I drove a truck, pumped gas, worked as an usher in a drive-in theatre, as a dishwasher, as a fry cook, worked on a road crew, in a door factory, and in a Coca-Cola bottling plant. I took whatever job I could find and was grateful for it. Now, fast-forward two score years 1995, when I was looking for a student to take care of weeding my yard. We posted ads at the high school and the college as well as the neighborhood grocery stores. We were looking for someone to pick their own hours and days so long as they kept the yard reasonably clear of weeds. There were *no* responses at $10 an hour, more than double the minimum wage. I would have been all over that offer during my school years, but none (not a single one) applied. This, which some might call a trivial incident, signaled to me a huge and disturbing shift in values and a worrisome trend for our country. It is out of my concern for our future competitiveness, our collective well-being and cultural dynamism that I feel the need to dedicate the time to putting my thoughts down on paper.

Over the years, I have been blessed to know and work with a number of leading-edge thinkers, both provocative and profound. These were individuals who were well ahead of the curve and who had a significant impact on my thinking. One of the earliest was the late Dr. George Steiner, economics professor emeritus at UCLA. Dr. Steiner's top-level positions in the federal government, including the dual posts of director of policy in both the Defense Production Administration and in the Office of Defense Mobilization in the Executive Office of the President of the United States laid the groundwork for what we have come to call long-range strategic planning. His books in this area are classics and, still today, among the most comprehensive on the subject of planning. As is so often the case, the key principles are simple yet enormously powerful, but the one that said the most to me was that "the purpose of long-range planning was to make better decisions today." Another individual I had the rare and special privilege and pleasure of knowing and who has also had a considerable and lasting effect on my thinking was the late Dr. Russell Ackoff. My deep interest in his ideas began many years ago with the reading of his 1984 book *Revitalizing Western Economies*, as well as his works on strategy, operations research, and organizational design. My respect for him and his thinking continues to grow in spite of his passing. It is not just his systemic approach that I find so universally powerful but his unfailing ability to see straight through to the core of the issue and separate the wheat from the chaff. Clearly these two qualities, his keen ability to connect the dots and, at the same time, see the fallacies of the obvious, are central to the principles embodied in the concept and application of non-zero-sum leadership.

Among other people who have influenced my thinking was Dr. Peter Drucker, and especially his early book *Concept of the Corporation* and, of course, his concept of managing by objectives. I was especially privileged to have his advice and counsel when founding the institute. Then there was the late Dr. George Odorine and, in particular, his book *Management by Objectives: A System of Managerial Leadership*, which popularized the concept and the process. The late Prof. Dale McConkey followed on with his book titled *Management by Results*, which took MBO to a new level. Dale was not only a seasoned senior executive but a consummate teacher as well. These were seminal books (and individuals) that sounded the closing bell on the preceding decades of scientific management. Today's *In Search of Excellence, Good to Great, The Reengineering Revolution, Seven Habits of Highly Effective People, The One Minute Manager, and Fish!* also give us pause to reflect on the meaning of organizational purpose and, hopefully, examining its responsibilities to its stakeholders in a rapidly changing global society. The good news is that these ideas get us thinking; the bad news is some don't have legs and tend to go out of fashion as organizations move from one to the next with increasing ease and with somewhat predicable results. Like boiling water, once the heat is turned down, the water settles back to its original state. This is not to suggest that these approaches don't have value, but by and large they ignore our fundamental human programming. They are based primarily on the notion that if "I can just get the organization (i.e., its people) to do *this*, we will reach a sustainable higher level of performance." The flaw in this thinking is that all these, to be successful over the long haul, involve a kind of cultural shift that requires a deep commitment to change not inherent (or natural) in most organizations today. Fundamentally, we are win-lose animals, and unless and until we do something about that, we will continue to be frustrated in our attempts to improve organizational performance by simply cutting employees. Moreover, managers have stood by, mostly on the sidelines, as all these initiatives have come and gone for decades as they know that this too will pass. What organizations need is to recognize that the only changes that work over the long run are those that are based more on the nature of people and less on the needs of organizations.

The individuals mentioned above (and others) along with their keen insights have helped to shape some of the key qualities of the non-zero-sum leader. One such principle is coming to understand that problems rarely, if ever, are isolated single time or place events. We need to make the time to explore the possibility that what we see could simply be a manifestation of a deeper systemic cause and should be first looked at in that way. This is why the integration of these two ideas—systems thinking and management by objectives—has so much potential power. The fusion of these two models produces something akin to *thinking by objectives*.

One important point in reading this book: while the examples are drawn from my personal experiences, I hope that you will see past that to the underlying principles of non-zero-sum leadership. I apologize for the lack of other-person experiences.

CHAPTER ONE

A Time for Reflection

> By three methods we may learn wisdom: First, by reflection, which is noblest; second, by imitation, which is easiest; and third by experience, which is the bitterest.
>
> —Confucius

Sometimes a Conversation with a Friend Can Help to Shape Our Thoughts

Is that you, Bob? Give me your hand and I'll help you up. Yes, it is a nice view from up here; the air has a certain crispness and the sun a bit more warmth. I also appreciate the fact that the horizon line extends far enough that you can just begin to see the curvature of the earth. It provides the perspective that helps one to recognize patterns, and that is a key element in separating an effective non-zero-sum leader from the zero-sum leader. I'm glad you stopped by. I enjoy sitting up here and reflecting on the issues and challenges of the day, and all the better to have someone to bounce ideas around with. I like to do it from this place because I don't need to find the forest through the trees because from up here, I can see over the top of the forest. Down there, no matter where I stand outside the box, I can't see very well around the box I just stepped out of because it impedes my vision. But then, Bob, as you were a navy pilot, you had the almost-daily experience of a thirty-thousand-foot view outside the box, so you can appreciate what it does for one's perspective. Grab a chair and I will get us a couple of beers from the cooler. So what do you think of this beer? I think it's pretty good too, especially considering the fact that it has absolutely no alcohol. No, it's not the so-called nonalcoholic 0.5 percent kind but a real 0.0 percent beer. Let me get some chips to munch on. You know, Bob, I've been writing this book that focuses largely on the leadership of people in a multidimensional way. The central questions I am posing are, what is non-zero-sum leadership, and does it make a difference? Does it optimize development and performance, and most of all, does it foster passion? The other dimension is the effect of generational changes and the impact of those methodological, technological, and societal changes on decision making and leadership. While politics may play a significant part in this process, I want to focus on the business aspects and the forces that work, in my opinion, to actually diminish (i.e., eat away at) our exceptionalism and our potential for greatness. What I have tried to do in this book is to revisit these decisions through a non-zero-sum lens. Frankly, Bob, what I see disturbs me. The stewards of our society, both in the political arena and in business, have made some decisions that I think won't (and some that clearly didn't) stand the test of time. I think Benjamin Franklin said it best. "All human situations have their inconveniences. We feel those of the present but neither see nor feel those of the future; and hence we often make troublesome changes without amendment, and frequently for the worse." This really gets to the core of my concerns. Have we made, and are we now making, the best decisions for our future?

A Case Study

Since the eighties, American goods production has been on a steep down slope, and with it America's middle class. Virtually all segments of the goods-producing sector, whether it is the steel industry, ship-building, textiles, major appliances, TVs, technology, the auto industry, and countless others, have all gone through (or are going through) major adjustments in order to stay competitive in this global economy. Many of these middle-class jobs have been completely outsourced to other countries and will never return to our shores. I think it is revealing to take a detailed look at how (and why) this metamorphosis happens over time. It reminds me of the caterpillar hiding itself from sight only to emerge completely changed as a butterfly without anyone taking note of or observing the change itself. For most of these industries, a detailed history of these changes is not readily available. However, the auto industry is an open book, and therefore, that segment of our industrial base is the best example for us to reflect on. I think the bottom line here is that unless (and until) we start thinking and acting in a more strategic, long-term way, the United States will continue down a slippery slope. It helps me to be up here where our vision is 360 degrees. What I see is that we are now in the midst of what I refer to as the Chinexico of America; our current generation of leaders are not simply undermining (selling off) our productive capacity but the obsessive focus on the "opportunities" in the Chinese market for U.S. companies seem to be *driving* us to make some questionable and compromising decisions that will come home to haunt us in the future.

A Deeper Look at What Is Going On in the Cocoon

Yes, I agree that a country with 1.3 billion people and a growing economy clearly offers big possibilities, and China has managed to fashion a controlled form of capitalism to further its economic, political, and military ambitions. It is, for example, currently estimated some 65.6 million households in China will soon have annual incomes of 60,000 yuan or more—a level deemed sufficient for a family to buy a no-frills car. It seems that estimate has caused Detroit to see an endless stream of dollar signs. That estimate, while interesting from a statistical point of view, *suggests* that if everyone in Manhattan who could *afford* to buy a car were to go out and buy one,

Manhattan would instantly become the world's largest parking lot. So being able to afford to buy a car does not necessarily mean that people will go out and buy one, yet I fear that is what Detroit takes from these numbers, and makes decisions accordingly. What Detroit is doing reminds me of the story of a young child who drowned in a river that averaged less than one foot in depth. Let me be clear, Bob, I think there are some very good reasons for America to be in that market. My concern is that which Benjamin Franklin posed, "Neither see nor feel those of the future." According to the China Association of Automobile Manufacturers (CAAM), vehicle sales in China in 2012 grew 4.3 percent to 19.3 million vehicles. Using my little out-dated handheld calculator, this would seem to indicate that (all other things being and staying equal) in 3.4 years, the market will be saturated. But before I go any further, I want to make clear that when it comes to numbers, they change almost daily. So what may be true as we are talking here today, Bob, may not be true tomorrow. But let's look at one example of how this thinking really transformed our country, albeit almost one hundred years ago. When Henry Ford decided to increase his workers' daily pay to $5.00, he did this, in part, so they could afford to buy the Model T they were building. To be historically correct, he did not simply raise their salaries but offered a bonus of an "extra" $2.50 a day if they met certain conditions, such as learning to speak English and if they did things the "American" way, i.e., they didn't drink or smoke. Women couldn't get the bonus unless they were single mothers, and men couldn't get it if their wives were also working. Nevertheless, taking this step meant that one of Ford's factory workers could buy a model T with roughly 100 days' pay. However, for the Chinese workers referred to in the consultant's analysis (making 60,000 yuan a year), that would translate into 150 days to buy *the cheapest* car (the GM plant in Liuzhou produces the Le Chi car priced as low as 40,000 yuan or $6,403). Now, Bob, bear in mind that there are already over 170 different car,

truck, and bus manufacturers in China. One such manufacturer (Tianqi Meiya) sold a total of seventy-seven cars in 2012 and others as little as a few thousand. Most of these are companies subsidized by  the Chinese government. Now stepping it up a bit, another GM car is available starting at 62,800 yuan ($10,080) equaling *over a year's annual salary*. By comparison, even today, the average U.S worker can buy a Dodge Dart with 152 days of earnings, whereas the Chinese worker, buying the "upscale" Baojun, has to work 230 days (the average U.S. working year is 220 days) to pay for it. Now if you had to pay a year's salary for a car, would you be replacing it every three to five years? I would expect the replacement cycle would be substantially longer than in the United States, and certainly not every three to five years.

A View through the Non-Zero-Sum Lens

So now we come to the key central question, what will these factories turn to once their output exceeds the demand? This is inevitable and sooner rather than later. I don't think the Chinese can long continue to subsidize these marginal operations as they are already starting to feel the financial consequences of unbridled "investments" in marginal activities. Moreover, there are already signs that the bloom may be off the rose. Armani opened a Chinese flagship store in 2004, hailing Shanghai as "the world's most talked about city." The store was recently shuttered. Hermès products are being sold secondhand by Chinese people who need cash. But China has a full-employment policy, so I don't think they will simply close down all these factories, and I also doubt that GM and Ford will simply walk away from their very substantial investments in China. I think they will do the same thing that Toyota, Honda, VW, and all the others have done: sell into the United States and other developed markets. In fact, in 2012,

Chinese exports grew by 19 percent to one million cars annually, primarily to the Middle East, Russia, and South America. In a recent interview, the head of China auto operations for one of the big two said when asked about exporting cars into the United States, "Since the U.S. imports cars into China, I don't see any reason not to have cars made in China exported to the U.S." This is, of course, exactly what the Germans and Japanese did after WWII after they had rebuilt their auto-making industry and, having satisfied the immediate regional demands, turned to the United States for continued growth.

The critical difference between then and now, Bob, is this picture above of the first Honda imported into the United States. That first Honda gave Detroit some time to retool to and compete, but even then, executives from the U.S. auto industry pleaded with the government to implement some trade restrictions that would make it less painful for them to catch up. Now, however, this car on the left is the car that could soon be seen in the U.S. showrooms for thousands of dollars less than virtually every car currently offered by Detroit. There is no room (or time) for catch-up given the fact that the United States can build cars in China for much less than it can in Detroit, and it may not make cents for them to even try to keep manufacturing here.

Cars like the Fiat 500 (MSRP $16,000) could potentially face competition from the Le Chi at something in the range of 50 percent less than the cost of the Fiat. For that matter, the Dodge SXT would be selling against the

Baojun 630 at something like 30 percent less than the Dodge, even after allowing for the added costs of transportation. I would expect the needed adjustments to come from factories in Detroit and not in China. Recently, the *Wall Street Journal* commented that we may see "high levels of overcapacity and significant margin pressure within the next three to five years," and Bill Russo (president of auto consulting firm Synergistics Ltd. and a former Chrysler executive) estimated that "China's overcapacity in three years could total 10 million cars, roughly equivalent to Japan's 2012 total auto production." Bob, I am not joking. Chinese cars! Yes, the Chinese are determined to build global brands. It is a matter of national pride and importance, a strategic decision already made by China. I can't help but muse why the Chinese haven't adopted as their new national anthem the Irving Berlin's 1946 song from *Annie Get Your Gun* "Anything You Can Do I Can Do Better." Or at the very least, cheaper.

You think they have a long way to go to develop the manufacturing skills necessary to pull this off? Remember, Bob, at this very time GM and Ford are training tens of thousands of workers in China to build world-class cars, so I think it is possible even now. GM has even built its new fuel technology research lab in China, and Ford is investing $5 billion in new plants, bringing its total to fourteen in China. I think David Roman got it right when he said the following:

> For the time being, many big companies with roots in China and other emerging markets are invisible to global consumers. However, the business success—brand momentum gap—and the time it has historically taken to grow a global brand—may be providing a false sense of security to some well-established brands in the West. As emerging market companies leverage their home court advantage and discover ways to appeal to the Net Gen, top global brands should pay careful attention to the shifting competitive landscape. A few years from now, I predict that an

increasing number of what are today unfamiliar
or exotic-sounding company names will become
not only big companies but truly global brands.

Roman's point being, in part, that social media now plays a
major role in building global brands; after all, how long did it take
for Facebook to become a global brand or LinkedIn or Twitter
or Google?

It may be that our government bailed out the automobile
industry (at a net loss of some $30 billion to the taxpayers), but the
rub is that "saving" the US auto industry resulted in putting Pontiac
and Saturn (America's grand experiment at producing quality cars at
more affordable prices) out of business. Hummer is now owned by
Sichuan Tengzhong, Land Rover and Jaguar (once owned by Ford)
are now owned by Tata in India, and Saab (once owned by GM) is
now owned by a Chinese consortium called National Electric Vehicle.
Now add to all that a loss of two thousand GM dealers and it seems
that saving the automobile industry did little to benefit Americans,
who lost 100,000 jobs as a result, and taxpayers lost billions. The
bad news only gets worse, and it is not just China Bob. GM has
spent $5 billion in Mexico, and Ford is building a new $2.5 billion
engine factory in Mexico with its 3,800 jobs. And finally, Bob, the
Jeep Renegade (an American icon) is now built by Fiat *in Italy* on a
Fiat chassis.

But hold on: like the Titanic, it's big and moving too fast. True
enough, as the service and technology sectors have become the dominant engines driving economic growth, this has presented us with
countless *new* opportunities along with some major challenges. Not
the least of which is that knowledge is highly portable, certainly at
much less cost and literally overnight, than are manufacturing operations. While it may have started with call centers, it clearly will not
end there. If one considers the outermost range of outsourcing, just
think about what it is that you *need* to do in one country versus
another. Jobs at fast-food outlets and the local gas stations are safe,
but not much else. If I want a hamburger, I don't want to travel to
India, China, or Poland to get one. On the other hand, if I need
something from a department store, I don't have to travel out of the

country as I can buy products made in the entire world's low-cost countries right here in America. This global dispersion of work will accelerate with unmerciful relentlessness. This is the take-no-prisoners march of global progress. We now find ourselves managing, more and more, remote and virtual resources. Indeed, there are now even firms that are themselves entirely virtual. It means we need to find new systems that fit this new reality and at the same time provide a high degree of stability and predictability. In this new context, organizations are faced with revisiting the way they manage their resources, especially people resources. However, given our historic (remember the cost of holding on to our outdated manufacturing base after WWII) fascination with the concept of sunk costs and organizational inertia, it may already be too late to change the course. Bob, I think you have a technical term for it: the radius-of-action formula or, as more commonly known, the point of no return. I was struck by Apple's recent decision to stop using certain harmful chemicals in its Chinese operations to protect its five hundred thousand(!) employees in their factories.

Chapter Two

In the Beginning

There was the word, and the word was *no.*

I just wanted you to have a little extra time to think about that.

As children, it is what and how we were taught. In part, this is understandable as humans don't come with instruction manuals, and even if they did, most of us would not take the time to read them. The fact that they don't come with manuals has created endless opportunities to engage in discussions about what the best way is to go about preparing children to take responsibility and to eventually become the best they can. My daughter's grade school had a newspaper, as did her high school, but there was none in the middle school. She felt the school should have one and went about trying to recruit her friends to help out. She didn't get any takers. At dinner one evening, she was again talking about how strongly she felt about the project, and I asked her, "Just how badly do you want to see this happen"? She said she felt very strongly about it, and so I advised her to do it herself and not to wait for someone else to make it happen. Sometime later, I found a jar on her bureau stuffed with $1 bills, and I asked where she got them. Turns out she had sold subscriptions to her (as yet unpublished) middle school newspaper to all our neighbors! She called the mayor, the police chief, the fire chief, and others and got interviews from all of them. She went on to have a high school column in the local newspaper, and during college, she even got a job as a radio news director and TV program manager.

Failing to tap into (or at least release) the natural spark or passion within almost all individuals is why we still have the discussion today; can people be taught to be leaders or is it in their genes? Picture all these potential future leaders in the context of the little boy I saw some time back who was wearing a T-shirt that said, "My name is not no no no." Leadership has as much to do with our programming as it does with our genes, desire, or ability. But I believe we too often assume that we are not part of that environment. After all, I had to step up just to start out on the bottom rung. By the time we get into the first grade, we understand, all too clearly, the nature of our zero-sum environments and have received extensive one-on-one instruction on the difference between winning and losing. More importantly, we also learn along the way that winning is a lot more fun, and it gets us the approval we seek from those we care about. If you have forgotten what the difference looks and feels like, just go to any Pop Warner or Little League game. On top of that, we are taught that winning is a "good" thing and losing is a "bad" thing. So by the time the leadership cream has risen, it is not improbable (or uncommon) that it has already hardened and the cheese has set. Our thinking patterns and habits are well entrenched, and absent some crisis or a driven visionary, chances are we are not very malleable at this stage. Can that be changed? Of course it can, but it takes a powerful desire, courage, and commitment.

This zero-sum paradigm is, in part, a fault of language. Western cultures are essentially reductive, and we tend toward zero-sum approaches to solving problems and expressing ourselves. Try this: as quickly as you can, after reading each word and without thinking about it, what springs to your mind? *Good…high…win…up… left…stop…gray.* My guess is that most of you thought *bad…low… lose…down…right…go,* and then you hesitated because *gray* has no obvious (zero-sum) opposite. Might *gray* be considered a non-zero-sum word? However, most of how we express ourselves is in zero-sum opposite terms. If we do tend to think in zero-sum terms, can we expect our life-shaping memories to be far behind?

Leadership is that way. Leadership is all about what is in our heads. My position is that leadership has a lot to do with genes and one's environment, but elements of it can be learned by various means. The point being that given the necessary genes, whatever inclination we might have had as a youth has been, whether by intention or not, unlearned or severely constrained. Studies have shown that it is more difficult for an experienced pilot to learn to fly a glider than a complete novice because a pilot must first unlearn (or compartmentalize) the old behaviors before they can learn the new ones.

Our world has been shaped by people of great vision, coupled with insatiable determination and inexhaustible patience and stamina. Some created new worlds, like Alexander the Great. Others created new countries, like Mohandas Gandhi. Others essentially created whole new industries, like Henry Ford and Andrew Carnegie. Others, like Konrad Zuse, gave us our first programmable computer, which changed our culture forever. Few of us can aspire to such greatness, but most of us have the capacity to set and achieve a greater us-ness.

A personal story may help you to discover what is possible in your world and what is central to non-zero-sum leadership. Not all goals can or need be of grand scale, but don't let timidity stop you from setting yourself some stretch goals. Let's see what opportunities lay buried below the clutter on your desk. In 1974, I had decided that I wanted to build a new organization dedicated to management and executive development. I knew, in advance, there were some things I did not want to do. By the way, therein lies a critical key to success in starting a business or running your lives, knowing what you want to do but, equally (perhaps more) important, knowing what you don't want to do. I knew that the approach had to be fundamentally different from everything that existed; it would be impossible to accomplish my goal using any model at hand. I wanted this new organization to be the very best, not the very biggest. That meant "inventing" a new model, as I had a very different cost-benefit model in mind. At that time, some would have it that it was not possible to be both differentiated and low cost; you had to be one or the other. The challenge was that I had in mind to find a way to be both.

For my purposes, I was focused on a specific set of factors, but for your purposes, it is the process that is of value in this exercise as it can be applied in virtually every situation. It starts with itemizing all the features that don't add value to your overall objective. In my case, the objective was learning. Let's start with the reasons (this is the core of the "why not" question talked about later in the book) that will not persuade one to attend a session that offers to make them a better manager or leader. Right off the bat, I am in Atlanta, but the session is in Los Angles. It is three days long, and I can't take that kind of time out of the office, and it costs several thousand dollars plus my travel expenses. I have no idea who the faculty will be, and equally important, I have no idea who the participants will be. Moreover, while the materials tell me that I will become more productive, it does not tell me what I can expect to learn in order to accomplish that. In other words, it leaves me to create my own set of expectations. The point of this analysis is to determine what it is that prevents achieving your goal, whatever that may be, whether in your own business, unit, department, office, or desk. What it is that prevents your day from being terrific. What it is that you invest your time and skill in doing that does not add value or clarity to your objective.

What was needed in my case was to completely eliminate, if possible, all the reasons (i.e., problems why) people don't go, or at least minimize those reasons. Since my focus was to build a learning organization that was the very best possible, that meant having the very best faculty possible, but it also had to be very cost-effective. It is important to understand that there are two types of classroom offerings to the general public. One is the generic training offering of the multiple-day type, and the other is the event type, which holds the session in a theater with hundreds in attendance. The latter is useful, in my opinion, essentially for cocktail conversation as you can impress your guests that you saw so-and-so without mentioning it was with the use of binoculars. When one looks at the costs that go into either of these public offerings, it turns out that 30 percent to 40 percent of the revenue is devoted to marketing and advertising. The first dilemma is, how do you spend 30 percent to 40 percent on advertising and offer the best faculty without raising your costs two- or threefold? I feel that if we offer the very best faculty, it follows that we can and shall be less dependent on advertising, so we eliminated all money for advertising, marketing, or sales to free up those funds to engage the services of the very best faculty. That is a bit risky as it requires inventing a whole new approach to reach your clients. The client then becomes the second issue to address. In order to provide the best possible learning experience, we need a mechanism to ensure an audience that is appropriate and reasonably homogenous. This means that we cannot simply open the doors to any and all comers but have to be selective in those that we will reach out to. The result is a members-only approach that allows us to focus on those organizations that will value and benefit from the type of learning we envision. This decision also enables us to overcome another short-coming of the public offerings, and that is selection of subject matter. Public offerings are decided at the head office based upon what *they* think will sell best and draw the biggest possible audience. As a members-only organization, we can reinvent the agenda every year to match what the members think is needed in each region, so every city has its own curriculum planning committee. The sessions need to be held where the members are and not where we are, and they must be in a single day. Some will question the one-day format, but I think the reason that most have three or more days is so they can charge more. We have found that if you have the right audience, the faculty can better focus on the material and thus cover a good deal more in one day than multiple days with an open-door policy. It also means inventing a new means of communicating since there is to be no advertising or marketing. We built a robust electronic delivery system that serves the needs of over 425 member organizations in six countries at no cost to them and very little to us. Another thing that had always troubled me was the cumbersome registration processes most public programs require and the penalties for cancelling within X number of days and, in particular, the onerous charges, some in the thousands, should you not show up on the day of the session. There are all sorts of arguments for doing this, and all are motivated by the expectation of increasing revenue. We decided that because we have a member base, and these are all very responsible organizations, they are unlikely to simply not show up not because it is a nice day for golf but rather that an emergency came up, and we will not punish them for events outside their control, so our organization has no charge (none) for cancellations or no-shows—even on the day of the session. No one is billed anything before the session, only afterward, and then only if they actually come. It also bothered me that public programs would cancel sessions if there were not *enough* registrations. This leaves those who had intended to come without the learning they had planned on (and presumably needed), and equally important, the faculty will have to find out a few days in advance that their session in Los Angeles is cancelled. You simply cannot ask the best faculty to bet on the outcome, and so our organization does not cancel sessions for lack of sufficient registrations—period. Members plan ahead, and if you ask them to communicate the offerings internally, the organizations, in turn, need to know you mean what you say. What I have tried to outline here is that by reframing the objective, indeed by looking at the root causes, it puts you in a position to reinvent what it is you do, why it is you do it, and how it is you do it.

So let's back up a little. All the evidence tells us that by the time children reach age eight, their life values and their programs are pretty much set. So what does that leave us with? If you haven't been to a preschool lately, you may have forgotten the natural leadership that comes with a child as part of the package, preassembled at the factory, so to speak. Still, we humans are social animals, and so we teach our children to "fit in" and "get along" as best we can. It starts with simple, seemingly harmless, and well-intended instructions. "Let Barry play with your toys, don't be selfish." "Let your sister have a turn." "Don't hog the ball." These do not, in and of themselves, void your child's leadership warranty, but keep it up and sooner or later, fitting in will become the dominant leadership style. Moreover, we are constantly surrounded at an early age with zero-sum situations, with games like jacks, hopscotch, baseball, board games, chess, volleyball, with being the lead in the school play, and into adulthood with golf, tennis, political office, who will be the next vice president of marketing, or whatever, and in all these, there is only one winner; the rest of us are, by definition and default, losers. It is a plain but ugly fact that if you choose to live in a zero-sum world, it is populated mostly with nonwinners. It is how we educate (socialize) our children, and for too many of us, we develop our managers using the same zero-sum approach. We spend way too much time on what not to do and way too little on what to do.

How does this manifest itself in the workplace? One example is the morning the swing shift manager of computer operations came into my office to inform me that he had to fire the data entry supervisor. I told him, "If that is what is needed to run his shift properly, then go ahead and do it." I did ask, however, that before he let her go, he should ask the "underperforming" supervisor to go home that night and write down what she thought the most important objectives (priorities) of her job were, and I asked him to do the same for her job. The next day, he came into my office and declared,

"Never mind, the problem is solved." Knowing what is expected can do wonders for an organization and the people in them. The point is that we spend way too much time unteaching (deprogramming) natural leadership and too little in developing that natural trait. Are all born with that gene? Of course not, but many more than make it to adulthood. It seems logical then that we can reignite that spark in most. In some cases, however, the early childhood training is just too successful. Zero-sum leaders often rely on the "I shouldn't need to tell them how" approach to managing. It is the way we were raised and the way we raise our children. We wait until they do something wrong and then tell them what they did wrong. But it is so much easier for employees to hit a target if they know where and what to look for. It is a little like playing with a model train—the only time we fix it is when it gets off the tracks. I am not talking about the "Be sure to tell them when they do a good job" gambit; I am talking about telling them what a good job would look like. I am not talking about goal setting but rather giving people the tools and insights to recognize what is wanted and needed to successfully meet the performance expectations of the job. It is about arming them with the knowledge and power (not *empowering* them, which is more often interpreted simply as giving them permission) to know at the end of the day that "I stayed on track." Most people really want to do a good job, but they need to know how that is defined, for how else will they know if they have achieved it?

Few people get ahead by losing. That is what zero-sum leadership is all about. It is making sure you are the plus one and not the minus one. The good news is that it is also what drives some to excel. It is what makes for successful entrepreneurs and champions. However, by the time we get into management positions, this drive to win can become less of an asset and more of a handicap. In fact, it goes a long way toward explaining why virtually all attempts to engage managers in some sort of "Let's share the winning [and losing]" has almost never worked. At some level, principally at the intellectual level, everyone understands it, but at the gut level, it just plain doesn't feel right. After all, *I* worked my way up by being "in charge" and being the best (i.e., the winner), and I am not about to now take on the role of letting someone else win, which my pro-gramming tells me makes me the loser. Being a successful leader is all about balance, having a healthy dose of drive (i.e., winning), but coupled with a genuine desire to bring about no losers. How is that possible, you ask?

If we give it some thought, there are actually at least two other ways of arriving at non-zero-sum outcomes other than win-win, which is not always possible and, in some instances, irrelevant. For example, you walk into a casino with $100 in your pocket, and two hours later (after spending that entire time at the slot machines), you leave the casino with exactly $100 in your pocket. Are you a winner or a loser? If not one or the other, by definition, it is not a zero-sum outcome; it is a non-zero-sum outcome. This is a core principle of non-zero-sum leadership, creating situations where being a nonloser or a nonwinner can be a more desirable outcome than one in which for every winner, you create a loser. The central idea is that if one is not a winner, it does not necessarily mean that the only option left is to be a loser. If you buy into this argument, then it follows that if someone wins and the other person is a nonloser, we have a non-zero-sum outcome. Indeed, another option is if both parties lose, we also have a non-zero-sum outcome. I know that sounds absurd, but just look at what goes on in politics to see how easy and often lose-lose outcomes happen—just count the number of bullet holes in the politician's shoes!

What is true is that the qualities of effective leadership share certain characteristics, but in the final analysis, it all boils down to the simple fact that leadership is a function and direct result of the decisions people make. We can (and will) spend the rest of this book talking about these leadership attributes. Think about all those you consider to be effective leaders and ask yourself why you see them so. You can start with Steve Jobs, George Patton, Ronald Regan, Bill Gates, Jack Welsh, Winston Churchill, and all the others who have impacted history in all its forms. Few of us will ever have the oppor-tunity to bring about change of this scale, but we will (and do) have the chance to make a measurable difference in those around us and those within our sphere of influence, but it takes vision, conviction, and courage.

So in starting, what are your goals? But remember what Prof. Dale McConkey said, "You can't do a goal." So what is your plan to reach those goals? What do you have to stop or start doing to reach your goal, whether at home or on the job? What is it that prevents your day (every day) from being perfect? Think about going to work tomorrow and everything is absolutely without any problems or issues. First off, how would you know that? Secondly, what would you look to for confirmation of what you think? Do you have all the information you need to know that all is well? This simple process (which we will explore in more depth later) forces you to focus on the doughnut and not the hole.

Chapter Three

Legacy Leadership

> Management is doing things right; leadership is doing the right things.
>
> —Dr. Peter Drucker

In this chapter, we will explore the merits (or demerits) of using rubber bands as predictors of the future. At one point, I was chairman of the strategic planning committee for a large food company. I had been asked by the president to put together short- and long-range plans for the company. As part of collecting the data I needed, I took one particular product about which I had some questions. I printed out a yearly sales volume chart for the past fifteen years. The numbers indicated an average growth rate of just over 2 percent per year. I took that information to the senior vice president of sales and asked him to circle every year that represented a year the company lost money on the product. He circled a half dozen or so years and indicated those were years the company lost a lot of money on that product. Now, taking those loss years out of the calculation, the sales on this new demand basis, the year-over-year sales were, in fact, a decline of almost 3 percent. You see, when we rely solely on the rubber-band approach to forecasting, it just predicts sales and not demand or profitability. In the bad years, the company did whatever they needed to do (reducing prices below the cost of production) to sell whatever they had in inventory. They achieved their sales goals, but try as hard as they could, volume did not make up for selling below cost.

In preparation for going further into the principal ideas of non-zero-sum leadership, I think it helps to frame the issues and the challenges by spending a little time on the factors that contributed to where we are today. Some industries have a term for the costs brought about by decisions made long ago and under very different circumstances; they call them legacy costs. For two decades, industries like autos, airlines, steel, ship building, and others have been struggling with these carry-over burdens in an effort to regain (some would argue gain) a sustainable competitive advantage in a global economy. This rearranging of the game board has cost hundreds of thousands (if not millions) of jobs and will doubtless cost hundreds of thousands more before the ship is righted. Some industries like shoes, textiles, TV manufacturing, and even toy manufacturing found it was easier (and more profitable) to just offshore rather than try to fix the problems. There is another legacy that has not received much attention and cannot be offshored, and that is legacy leadership. After all, the decisions that lead to the current situation were not made in a vacuum and certainly not by the workers. Let's take a few steps back to put today's organizational challenges into their historical context. Indeed, why is it we need to change anything, let alone ourselves or our view of the world or our organizations? Whatever we did worked well for a very long time, what is it that is so different now?

The generation following the end of WWII (1945–1965) enjoyed an enormous advantage. We could do no wrong; the United States was the unchallenged leader of the industrialized world. No other country even came close. Whatever (and however) the United States produced its goods and services, they would and could be profitably sold. This mind-set made for some careless decisions as companies were using the rubber-band approach to forecast well into the future. Union contracts based on a seemingly endless string of ever-increasing production of goods, services, *and* profits were largely responsible for creating the legacy costs so often blamed for the decline (and lost jobs) of the eighties and nineties. For the most part, costs were not a major concern during this period because the other potential major players were busy rebuilding their infrastructure after WWII and not in a position to challenge America's dominance in the market. Moreover, the United States had abundant and cheap natural resources. It also helped that the U.S. workers were the most productive in the world thanks in part to Frederick Taylor, who published his ground-breaking *Scientific Management* work in the steel industry in 1911. His work, which focused mainly on what Taylor called soldiering in the steel industry (i.e., shoveling pig iron) and bricklaying, had spillover applications in non-manual-labor areas. Many U.S. companies employed scientific management techniques, time management practices, and piecework pay throughout this period in an effort to make best use of labor and maximize profits. Taylor's work had an enormous impact on productivity and helped America gain a competitive foothold that resulted in commanding advantages in the marketplace. Taylor's methods, however, were seen by some as dehumanizing, which eventually resulted in an investigation by the United Stated Congress. Nevertheless, many forms of Taylorism can still be found in factories and (yes) offices today. Scientific management didn't die with Taylor but spilled over into other disciplines. At the end of WWII, a group of ten unemployed air force statisticians (later to be known as the Whiz Kids) led by their commanding officer, Charles "Tex" Thornton, approached Ford with a proposal to use their considerable skills to modernize Ford's management. One member of this group was Robert McNamara, who later became the first non-Ford family member to become president of the company and was later recruited by President Kennedy to be secretary of defense. At that time he was lionized as the very model of the star business executive. I would argue that this approach of "management by the numbers" signaled the first (albeit small) crack in United States dominance of the world markets. Ford now began to focus on efficiency and cost savings with a vengeance (none of the Whiz Kids had any production, marketing, or sales experience), and the primary focus was, in effect, how to replace steel and aluminum with plastic. The Ford Falcon is considered McNamara's contribution to the world of auto making. With the emphasis on the numbers at Ford, others started to follow. U.S. auto companies were trying to accommodate the changes in U.S. consumer demand for bigger but less expensive (and more profitable) cars, thus expanding the market and their share of it. By the late sixties, other countries were busy rebuilding their auto making capabilities and looked to the United States to provide the market for their growth. While the United States turned out cars like the Ford Falcon, the Chrysler Valiant, Chevrolet Corvair, the Studebaker Lark, and the AMC Rambler, others were preparing to challenge them with cars such as the Volkswagen Beetle and the Volvo, soon to be followed by Honda and Toyota.

I don't believe that the Untied States, or the Whiz Kids, deliberately set out to make inferior cars. These automobiles were designed to meet an expanding market demand for less costly cars. In fact, I owned a Falcon and a Corvair, and they were decent cars. In context, however, these cars, and the dominant position of the United States at that time, had some unintended consequences. The long-term impact of these factors and others led the United States to make some critical and very costly misjudgments. Using a rubber band to project future sales never works, and that was what the United States was doing during these formative years. Simply stretching out a straight line along the historical data points as far as the rubber would stretch. It was this mind-set, along with one other major factor (discussed in the next chapter), that set the stage for the implosion of many of the major industries in the United States.

The central fallacy in the rubber-band approach is that it leads one to think that sales growth is the same as demand growth (and profits) and will continue into the future along their past path. The dark side of this as applied to U.S. growth after WWII was that we did not take into account the fact that, at some point, Europe and Japan would finish rebuilding their infrastructures and turn to producing products that would necessarily rely heavily on exports. The facts are that the German home market had been depleted by 3.2 million military personnel and 3.8 million civilians killed during the war. I lived in Germany in the midfifties when the VW Beetle was staring to roll off the production lines. The domestic model had painted bumpers and mechanical brakes, but the export model (destined for the United States) had chrome bumpers and hydraulic brakes. The export market was critical to Germany's (and Japan's) economic growth and prosperity. Poland was close behind with 6.9 million lost, Japan lost 2.8 million, Britain lost 449,000, and the United States lost 418,000. So we allowed ourselves to block out this inevitable transition as Europe and Japan would quickly saturate their domestic markets and would turn to America to build and sustain their economies.

This lulled us into a cost-and-competitive trap from which we have not recovered and likely never will. If we look at any industry or business, we can generally divide costs into two main categories: variable and fixed. Essentially, fixed costs are those you pay even if you don't open the doors. Variable costs are those that move up (or down) depending on demand, production levels, and profits. Everyone thought things would continue as they had in the past when increases in profits would be seen (by unions) as excess capital that should be shared by the workers. This was a perfectly understandable and reasonable approach—at that time. However, unlike Congress, industries cannot raise capital by voting for it. This was where the devil in the details set the United States on the road to disaster. The "sharing" of these seemingly endless profits eventually resulted in ever-higher wage rates; inefficient and costly union work rules; increasing job security, which meant less flexibility as conditions changed; and expensive fixed retirement and health benefits. Simply put, this means that if production declines, you still pay basically the same costs per unit, as though production had not declined. Instead of agreeing to unrealistic and unsustainable wages and benefits, these industries would have been much better off using the economic value of the work as the basis for pay and coupling that with a profit-sharing plan. That would have meant that when times were good, workers would share in a portion of the profits, and some would be set aside by the company for worker retirement benefits. It could even have meant workers might have done better when profits were up (a "novel" incentive), but costs would have, in any event, represented the value of the work rather than the number of years a particular individual had performed the work. What is the value of installing a car door? Should it double by using a worker who has twenty years seniority versus a new person on the line? By holding to pay for value, when production (business) fell off, the fixed costs would have been at a manageable level. It is axiomatic in business that you keep fixed costs as low as possible, a cardinal rule ignored at that time by both industry and the unions. Now the very survival of companies, whole industries, and even our country rests on their ability to undo fifty years of shortsighted rubber-band policies.

There were other contributing factors, which will be discussed in the next chapter, but the bad news is that it didn't (and won't) get any easier. Yet we were provided ample warning. In 1976, Dr. Daniel Bell of Harvard published his book titled *The Coming of Post-Industrial Society*. In his groundbreaking work, he described the USSR and the United States as the only two industrialized nations. The dichotomy between the two was the capitalist and the collectivist mind-sets. He correctly foresaw the essential attributes of the postindustrial capitalist society, such as the diffusion of global capital, the imbalance of international trade, and the decline of the manufacturing sector on the U.S. domestic front. Equally important, he emphasized that changes to postindustrial society are not just social, structural, and economic. The values and norms within the postindustrial society change as well. Rationality and efficiency become the paramount values within the postindustrial society. According to Dr. Bell, these values will eventually cause a disconnect between social structures and culture. Most of today's unique problems can generally be attributed to the effects of the postindustrial society. These problems are particularly pronounced where the free market dominates. They can include economic inequality, outsourcing of domestic jobs, etc. Dr. Bell's analysis is now almost four decades old, or before over 50 percent of the U.S. population was born.

The generation between 1965 and 1985 came to leadership roles with a different vision and mind-set. This generation was rooted in the past but faced a very different world than their parents did. Their solutions tended to be awkward, tentative, and indecisive and lacking a long view. After all, we were being inundated by products made in other countries—and good products. I remember as CFO of a food company that was a major player in canned tomatoes, the Italians were just starting to import canned tomatoes into the United States, and I asked what our counterstrategy was, and the answer was…we had none. The same could be said of the automobile industry; they too had none. Many corporations are still struggling with these profound changes in an effort to realign structures and strategies to deal with and maintain profitability during these changes.

The next generation (1985–2005) came to maturity amid a very different set of circumstances. For the most part in the previous generation, we tended toward trying to upgrade outdated products, processes, and infrastructures, but those efforts were not enough to overcome the tide and determination of foreign competitors. The United States was facing increasing competition from abroad from companies that operated on a global scale, while most American companies were still operating in the multinational mode and had not yet morphed into true global organizations. The good news was that despite a series of negative shocks that began with the bursting of the NASDAQ bubble in 2000 and continued through the current spike in energy prices, U.S. productivity growth had remained vigorous and, in recent years, has even accelerated. Indeed, the U.S. economy has not enjoyed such sustained productivity growth since the 1960s. Because this generation had limited experience dealing with the competition on such a vast scale, our reactions were slower and less aggressive than they might otherwise had been. It was during this generation that the creation of manufacturing jobs started to turn south.

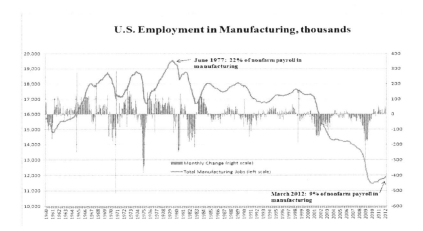

U.S. Employment in Manufacturing, thousands

Now we come to the current generation of leaders (2005–2015) when virtually all we knew (and had counted on since the end of WWII) is now turned on its head. Change now happens at warp speed. It is no longer enough to compete globally; we must *be* global. GE has trimmed its U.S. workforce by one fifth and shipped almost thirty thousand jobs to China. GM now has eleven plants in China and is building its new research center there. Apple employs five hundred thousand in China, manufacturing all its i-products there (at an average wage of 0.51 cents per hour), and the list of companies operating in countries outside the United States continues to grow. Can there be any doubt that these concessions won't come back in the next ten years to bite us? GE has already partnered with a Chinese airplane manufacturer whose targets are Boeing and Airbus. The United States is in a full-court press racing toward an economy based on Chinese manufacturing and sales. But this set of leaders is going ("a giant step for mankind") further than any of those before them. China is insisting on (and getting) as part of any joint deal that all the U.S. partners give them their technology. GE has turned over all their nonmilitary avionics to China, and GM has turned over all their automotive technology. I do believe there are sound reasons for much of this expansion of our U.S. global footprint, not the least of which is the market is some five times larger than the U.S. market and growing at three to four times faster. It just makes sense for American companies to have a significant presence there, and it will eventually follow that India will become an important market, per-haps in the next generation. But this globalization is not all one way. Toyota has six plants in the United States, Honda has four plants in the United States, and numerous other foreign companies have substantial operations in the United States, some operating under their U.S. labels. Some of these operations are primarily a function of (much) lower costs of production and, in many cases, much lower tax rates. For others, transportation costs are a major advantage to manufacturing abroad. Business-friendly environments outside the United States are yet another reason. For example, in China, the corporate income tax standard rate is 25 percent, but the tax rate could be reduced to 15 percent for qualified enterprises thiat are engaged in industries encouraged by the Chinese government (e.g., new/high-tech enterprises and certain integrated circuits production enterprises). Tax holidays are also offered to enterprises engaged in encouraged industries. In addition to China and India, the former Eastern bloc countries are beginning to flex their manufacturing and economic muscles. Absent a serious examination of our structural government regulations, subsides, robust public assistance programs and tax policies, the United States will not only continue to see its manufacturing base erode but will find itself alongside countries like Greece and Spain. Why is it that the *only* solution we seem to be able to come up with is to let thousands of U.S. workers go and replace them with workers in places like China, India, and Mexico? How is it that selling hamburgers is more secure and profitable than making cars? Could it be that what America needs is more nonlosers?

CHAPTER FOUR

The Thousand Days

> Being busy does not always mean real work. The
> object of all work is production or accomplish-
> ment and to either of these ends there must be
> forethought, system, planning, intelligence, and
> honest purpose, as well as perspiration. Seeming
> to do is not doing.
>
> —Thomas A. Edison

The late sixties and early seventies gave us our first peek
of the changes to come on
the path to a globalized economy. Previously we had international and even multinational organizations, but now
we were moving to a whole
new game board. Signs of growing sophistication in technology
began to hint at a closing of the gap between the United States and
its emerging global competitors. The Soviet Tupolev Tu-144 (pic-
tured above) became the very first commercial aircraft to exceed

Mach 2 and the Soviet Union landed Lunokhod 1 on Mare Imbrium (the Sea of Rains) on the moon. This was the first roving remote-controlled robot to land on another world and was released by the orbiting Luna 17 spacecraft. The North Tower of the World Trade Center was topped out at 1,368 feet, making it the tallest building in the world. China's first satellite (Dong Fang Hong 1) was launched into orbit using a Long March-1 rocket (CZ-1), and China tested an atomic bomb in Lop Nor. American Motors Corporation introduced the Gremlin and Ford unveiled the Pinto. Japan introduced the Toyota E10 in 1966 and Honda followed in 1969 with its N600 with 354cc engine rated at 35–45hp. Paul McCartney announced that the Beatles had disbanded, and Elvis Presley died in 1977. It is a tribute to American resilience that we made it through that decade.

With all this and more going on, the United States was focusing on finding new ways to substitute plastic for steel and chrome. The rubber band was still the principle instrument for predicting the future, and why not? The past (up to that point) had been pretty good to us and for us. Neither the concept nor the potential impact of confusing variable with fixed labor costs had yet caught up with industry. It seemed that the changes due to the gradual maturing of certain markets and the shifting generational and cultural values were essentially ignored as, at that time, the overriding assumption was there existed an insatiable demand for American products and services. Now, as so often happens, the government stepped in to hammer the final nail. In 1970, the U.S. rate of inflation was 5.84 percent, and this so alarmed the Nixon administration that they decided they needed to stem this tide of inflation and imposed, in 1971, a ninety-day wage and price freeze.

This was not our first try at wage and price controls. America used them as early as 1630, when diminishing job opportunities and rising wages in Massachusetts Bay prompted the court of assistants to cap wages for several categories of skilled workers and for common laborers in general. During the American Revolution, some colonies also imposed a maximum wage in the building trades because of labor shortages. Then, in October of 1942, the Emergency Stabilization Act was passed, which placed wages and agricultural prices under control. Since organizations could not offer higher wages, they, instead, offered nonwage incentives to attract needed employees. Indeed. this was the major factor in employers beginning to offer a range of such fringe benefits as pensions, medical insurance, paid holidays, and paid vacations. Since these were not paid out in cash, they did not violate the wage ceiling. Then, in 1945, President Truman decided to relax the price controls. He issued a new executive order in October 1945 that made it easier for businesses to cover wage increases through higher prices. If wage increases pushed business profits below OPA profit standards, it authorized the agency to allow the affected business to raise prices. Still, this did little to calm the waters. During this period, the UAW struck against General Motors. It lasted for 113 days. Walter P. Reuther, representing the UAW, asked for both a 30 percent increase in wages and *no* increase in the prices of GM automobiles. Then, in January 1946, while the GM strike continued, steel workers struck United States Steel to press their demand for higher wages. No longer bound by their wartime no-strike pledge, workers increasingly turned to strikes to overcome owner resistance to wage increases. Between V-E and V-J days, the number of worker days of idleness due to strikes averaged less than 2,000,000 a month. In September of 1945, the total rose to 4,300,000. In October, it jumped again to nearly 9,000,000. In November, 180,000 autoworkers in GM plants went out, and over the next three months, so did many other workers, including those employed in meatpacking, electrical, and steel. By February of 1946, the monthly total worker days on strike reached 23,000,000, and we were off to the races.

In Nixon's case, the ninety days turned into one thousand days. The administration's actions did, in fact, change the rate of inflation. By 1974 (at the end of the one thousand days), the inflation rate had gone from 5.84 percent, when wage and price controls were imposed, to 11.03 percent, when they were finally lifted. As is so often the case, the law (while arguably well intended) actually sowed the seeds of America's industrial and competitive decline. The fatal flaw was that the law *did* allow for price increases in certain circumstances. For example, if you had a union contract, you were permitted to honor those and petition the government for a price increase of like percentage. In other words, if you could prove that your labor costs had risen, you could (and basically the only way you could) increase your prices. The U.S. industry was now, effectively, on a cost-plus basis. If you could prove your labor costs went up 5 percent, you could raise your prices. Since labor is never 100 percent of your costs, the difference (nonlabor costs) flows through into profits. As an example of how this worked in practice, I remember one executive committee meeting I sat in during the early part of this freeze. The main purpose of the meeting was to discuss the wage increases for the coming year, and the human resources executive said they would be approximately 6 percent higher. I anticipated a discussion would follow along the lines of "What can be done to moderate these increases?" Those discussions never took place as this increase was the company's only way to increase its profits. So as early as the seventies, we began to think of increased costs as something of no great consequence and, indeed, a blessing in disguise. Since there was essentially no serious foreign competition at that time and you have a customer base that is willing to pay the price, the focus shifted from producing quality products and services at the best possible cost to beating the system. So far so good as the war had decimated the rest of the industrial world, but that was not to prove to be a steady state.

During much of this period, other nations were focused on rebuilding their infrastructure. These countries had several (later to prove major) advantages over the United States. Since World War II had destroyed much of their infrastructure, these countries had clean slates to work with and to rebuild using only the very newest technology. While the United States continued to milk it's existing (WWII) manufacturing infrastructure, other countries literally leaped ahead. Not expecting (or used to) competition from outside, the United States continued to rely on its invested base. This was made all the more rational because America, at that time, enjoyed almost unlimited and inexpensive access to what was thought (or at least appeared) to be boundless natural resources, including oil. America naively believed that our industrial dominance would (1) never end and (2) was solely (at least largely) a function of our ability to outperform and outproduce any other nation. Equally important, from a competitive point of view, these other countries used this opportunity to rebuild their organizational structures, while America had the advantage of hanging on to its organizational roots, which had served it well during the war. It has been said that it is more often our successes that cause us problems than it is our failures, and this was no less true than in the three decades after the war. These "successes" would come back to haunt America in the eighties and nineties and would ultimately cost America hundreds of thousands of jobs. Beginning as early midsixties, America had begun to develop small cracks in its industrial base, and by the eighties, these cracks had become chasms. In the final analysis, we learned, painfully, that one country's advantage can become another country's opportunity.

Then, about this same time, the U.S. steel industry began its own implosion due in large part to the fact that the Japanese competition based its new steel industry on the latest (and superior) BOP technology. This was followed on closely by the decline of the U.S. ship-building industry for many of the same reasons. However, not all the reasons were related to old technology. This was the period in U.S. industrial history when it began to layer on what the United States now calls its legacy costs. The United States had gone through almost a three-decade-long period of inattention to the basics. Coinciding with strong demand was the growth of strong unions, and companies were not in the best position to make convincing arguments for cost restraint. We tend to think of this as a phenomenon unique to the auto industry, but it was throughout and touched virtually every industrial and service sector. Airlines had been protected by government fare regulations until fairly recently, and in order to survive deregulation have had to implement a multilevel wage program. It touched clothing, electronics, and almost any sector you can think of. Now America and its stakeholders are paying a very steep price for this negligence. In all fairness, this conflagration came about as a result of strong unions with short time horizons and with an "I want mine now" mind-set. I truly believe the course set had as much to do with building a strong union power base as it did with promoting and protecting the interests of the workforce. Moreover, adding to the challenges, industries struggled with the many union work restrictions that were supposedly designed to protect these very union jobs. Actually, these restrictions were more likely designed to expand the base by artificially creating more jobs for more workers by limiting what one worker could do, and really had little to do with protecting the worker. The case of the New York union roofer comes to mind as a classic example of such overcontrol by unions. A union roofer was prevented from doing more than the daily union-fixed number of roof squares even though he could, and wanted to, lay more. The union went to court, and the court upheld the union's right to set *maximum* work standards.

This went under the category of job protection. I remember an article some years ago where ten major company CEOs were interviewed, and one of the questions asked was what their toughest decision had been. Nine of the ten answered, "Letting those thousands of people go." So much for job protection. If unions had worried as much about creating jobs as they did about protecting them, the workers would be far better off today, and so would the United States. Righting the system will take time and will be painful for many. Untangling the sins of the past sixty years would be much easier if we start using shorter rubber bands lest we repeat the mistake of Samuel Vauclain, chairman of the board of Baldwin Locomotive, when, in 1930, he stated in a speech that "advances in steam technology would ensure the dominance of the steam engine until at least 1980."

It is not as though we weren't given ample time to prepare ourselves for global competition and to get our houses in order. After all, it was in 1976 that Dr. Daniel Bell published *The Coming of Post-Industrial Society*. Yet even today we have trouble seeing around the corners. Whether it is organizational and/or political planning, the failure is not giving adequate attention to the long-term systemic consequences of our actions. In different contexts, there are different criteria for what qualifies as sound knowledge and judgment. Science still makes use of a traditional understanding of knowledge, which derives from Enlightenment thinking. This relies on objective experimentation, logical deduction, and reductive thinking. However, this approach cannot be used with success when dealing with complex systems. Complexity theory realizes this, but much of the work done in complexity reverts to the traditional reductive criteria. In mathematics, especially in the area known as module theory, a semisimple module (or completely reducible module) is a type of module that can be understood easily from its parts. Unfortunately, few strategic problems can be effectively treated by reductive reasoning, and worse yet is the fact that we still continue to approach complex problems limiting our solutions by employing reductive thinking, which very often leads to unintended consequences.

Now we fast-forward to the twenty-first century. Corporations are still struggling with these profound changes in an effort to realign organizational structures and strategies to deal with (and profit from) the global evolution that gets all the more complex as, in addition to China, India, Mexico, and the former Eastern bloc, countries begin to flex their manufacturing and economic muscles. The good news is that despite a series of negative shocks that began with the bursting of the NASDAQ bubble in 2000 and continuing through the spike in world energy prices, productivity growth has remained robust and, in recent years, has even accelerated. Productivity gains have come both from the technological progress in the industries that produce IT equipment and software and the ongoing shift toward purchases of these newer technologies that are relatively cheap and highly cost-effective.

With all our successes (and there are many examples), what is it that makes us so slow to respond to global competition? Why is it that the only solution we seem able to come up with is to let thousands of workers go? After all, there are only so many openings for computer technicians. How is it that selling hamburgers is more profitable than making cars?

CHAPTER FIVE

What Is a Picture Worth

> Life consists not simply in what heredity and environment do to us but in what we make out of what they do to us.
>
> —Harry Emerson Fosdick

What we can glean from these first few chapters is that leadership has not only a contextual component but a historical one. Leadership values are largely inherited, and as values go, so go our perceptions, and following closely behind is our leadership style and, for many, their worldview. This was true of the future leaders born in the 1930s and 1940s.

Do you see your father or someone you know in this picture? Do you think these children grew up with a very different set of values than those of the last two generations? Do you think that the children of these children had a different set of values than the last two generations? Most likely even their grandchildren were affected.

It is likely that you, perhaps the child of Depression-era parents, were able to do things for your children that your parents could not even dream of doing for you and you have done (or will do) for your grandchildren. Don't you think that had an effect on the values of each successive generation, their vision of the world and their feelings? These values clearly had an impact on them and their worldview. It shaped their expectations, their beliefs, their drive, and their vision of who they might someday strive to be.

So given this largely environmental/parental framework, the age-old central leadership question persists, are leaders born or can leadership be taught? Well, the Depression has been over for seventy years, and as far as I know, there is no (economic) Great Depression gene to be passed on. So we must allow for these values and feelings to be passed on in some other form, the form of words. Arguably, the single most influential event in the past century was the Great (being of the period, I think it is better called the Deep as there was nothing great about it at all) Depression. Then, within a single generation, the situation was essentially inverted in a fundamental way. Yet the lessons and values taught during the Depression have, to a greater or lesser extent, been passed down from generation to generation to this day. Leadership is that way. Leadership is all about what is in our heads. Indeed, while we often ascribe our values and feelings to other parts of our body than our head, they are really stored in only that one organ. I know it sounds better to give a card that says "I love you with all my heart" than one that says "My neurons are stimulated by you," but the latter is the fact, the former the fiction. For that matter, a gut feeling is more often than not simply gas. The point being, it is what we carry around in our heads that makes a leader. Unfortunately, some of what we store away there is irrelevant and actually operates to impair and thwart our natural leadership abilities and traits.

My position is that leadership has an important genetic component, but the environment plays a big part in realizing its genetic potential. Gifted persons born in some remote area and without access to stimulating developmental opportunities have the odds stacked against them. On the other hand, a less-gifted individual given all the opportunities to reach full potential has a better chance of achieving success as a leader. Although genetics are a key building block, there is not a lot we, as individuals, can do to change that (at least not at the present time), so the rest of this book will focus on that which we can and do control.

Let's start with a basic assumption. I think anything that we can unlearn can be taught. It does not, however, mean that it will be learned, a notion we will talk about more in this book. It is not entirely clear to me whether it is more difficult to unteach than to teach. For as Henri Matisse said. "There is nothing more difficult for a truly creative painter than to paint a rose, because before he can do so he has first to forget all the roses that were ever painted." We earlier talked about how it is more difficult for an experienced pilot to learn to fly a glider than a complete novice because an experienced pilot must first unlearn (or at least compartmentalize) the old behaviors (i.e., training) before they can learn the new ones. Now let's look at what this means in our everyday development. All the evidence tells us that by the time a child reaches age eight, their life values (and to a great extent their behaviors) are pretty much set. So what does that leave us to work with later in life? Remember those natural leaders in that preschool we visited earlier. In the final analysis, the *only* person that can change your behavior is you. People learn and change when *they* want or need to, not always when *you* want them to. What makes them want to? Fear, opportunity, rewards, onward and upward, security, status, maybe even a parking space, in fact, almost everything other than teaching. You must have a motivated learner for teaching to be effective and lasting, at least if the objective is to produce a change in behavior. I taught information systems in college for a short while, and it was a lot more rewarding (and fun) to teach night school students because they knew why they were there. Not all day students knew, other than that they needed the course to graduate. Give me a compelling reason to learn and I will be all over it. For very few, it is the sheer joy of learning, but for others, a change in behavior may be taken as a threat to self. As teachers, we often delude ourselves into thinking that those assembled are (and want to be) learners. Teaching leadership needs an open and receptive mind. A Peters's axiom: "Teaching and fishing have one thing in common. Until the hook is set it is an academic exercise." Some suggest (believe) that everyone wants to be a leader. Not so. A study, some many years ago, by Dr. Sterling Livingston at Ford Motors found that 40 percent of all the managers he interviewed said that had they known what was involved in being a manager, they would not have taken the promotion.

Let's fast-forward a decade or so and see if just maybe these efforts are reflected in our mental leadership pictures of how we catalog people and behaviors. A situation that results in a winner and a nonloser (for now, just take as fact there can be such a thing as a nonloser) is a non-zero-sum outcome, as to be zero-sum, there must be opposites to cancel out. If we can agree on this, it opens a whole new way to think about our leadership. If we can see possibilities that create winners but no losers, it gives us another set of tools and options. Moreover, thinking in this way, it is possible to see the shortcomings of many of the approaches organizations have been using to ratchet up productivity and profits. In the last ten years or so, the basic strategy has been the classic squeeze play. Because time is *the* most limiting resource, this approach is understandable. Do what needs to be done, and we can rethink it later. Don't do it and there may be no later.

Organizations have, of course, tried numerous approaches to increase productivity and improve their competitive positions, for the most part without a great deal of success. Thirty years ago, it was participative management, and then came along intrapreneurship and then empowerment, and now slash-and-burn. The largely unsuccessful attempts to get buy-in (and more productivity) from employees are a good example of how little we factor in the human condition as a systemic component of our change process. For example, by its very definition, *empowerment* creates at least one loser. On the surface it is an intriguing notion, and most of us can buy into it at the intellectual level, but it is quite another thing to implement it at an organizational level. After all, empowerment means "to *give* somebody power or authority" or "to *give* somebody a sense of confidence or self-esteem." *Giving* someone else power or authority is often seen as taking away (i.e., you now have less), and we are programmed to see that as losing, and that is not a desired end state. While we can all agree that empowerment sounds like a desirable thing for the organization, its flaw is that it *costs* the empowerer, and this is why, in my opinion, it has never really caught on. Moreover, to be effective, the empowerer must first be comfortable with his or her own vulnerability and come to grips with the notion that power and respect, like love, grows *only* when you give it away. In my experience, this does not describe a characteristic of most managers and leaders. Therefore, lacking some kind of transformative experience, the problem is that as an organizational strategy, it is flawed.

In recent years, something like empowerment has been seen in organizations, but it is more a matter of the *taking on* of responsibility when all the old options are no longer available or viable. This phenomenon has come about by the implosion of organizational resources (combined with or as a result of other-sourcing), and this functions as one of the principal strategies for dealing with global competition. But as we pass through these functional and structural stages, we must consider the long-term effect of their larger and more fundamental societal and systemic impact. It is not a simple matter of reorganization, repositioning, retraining, or redundancy. Indeed, as we have moved through these stages, we have learned some important lessons, and those have shaped our leadership approach. But the future holds some very different challenges for American leadership, and past experience is only useful if you expect your future to look the same as your past. A recent statement pointing out (proudly) that "we are no longer a nation that makes things but a nation of ideas" is a statement I find absolutely chilling. If we take up that banner, it will lead the country further down the path to second or third place in the world economy. American exceptionalism rests largely on collective pride. We take pride in the Golden Gate Bridge, in the Empire State Building, the St. Louis arch, in our space program. We take pride in who we are as a nation, what we can accomplish with our can-do entrepreneurial spirit. A nation cannot take collective pride in an idea but only one that, by building on a foundation of ideas, creates demonstrable results.

We are further diminishing our collective pride by sacrificing cultural correctness on the altar of political correctness. It is hard (if not impossible) for a county (or an organization) to coalesce by discarding the melting pot in favor of a stew where, no matter how long it cooks, the carrot, meat, and potatoes will never come together. Said another way, an organization (or for that matter a country) cannot sustain itself without *cultural* correctness (i.e., cohesiveness built upon its core values), whereas the expedient of political correctness divides and weakens both. Our reckless abandon of the sound and important lessons of the thirties, forties, and fifties from our grandparents and parents have led us to a "This too will pass" attitude in both our organizations and our country. Further to the subject of moving the cultural needle I have lately come to wonder about the makeup of the recent violent protesters which resulted in looting businesses, burning cars and buildings, and deaths and have asked myself the question "how many of these protesters were vets"? Drafted out of college for two years of service I and my fellow recruits learned a lot about discipline, self-respect, respect for others, duty, and above all the importance of responsibility toward and for others. With some 40 percent of children living in homes with a single parent (most often a female) I can't help but wonder if they were afforded different role models could it make a difference? Maybe some 18 months in service (many countries offer the option of military or state service) would make a difference in their lives and ours. The fact is, it will not pass but grow evermore destructive and burdensome unless our leaders can stand apart from the immediate (and the often reactive) and begin to think in a more strategic way. Perhaps a small step in that direction may be non-zero-sum leadership.

Chapter Six

Talking about Words

> There are risks and costs to action. But they are
> far less than the long range risks of comfortable
> inaction.
>
> —John F. Kennedy

Among the many people who have influenced my thinking, the late Dr. David Berlo is on my short list. David had a clarity about communications and relationships that was both unique and powerful. Central to his thinking was his concept of "I mean you no harm" and its impact on one's leadership effectiveness. This becomes all the more important when coupled with the notion of non-zero-sum leadership. The concept is simple enough to understand but difficult to practice. The concept is that unless people (truly) believe that you mean them no harm, you will never get their full commitment and certainly never release their energy and potential.

This journey is about who we are, reflecting on how we got to be who we are, and reexamining the programming that is now part and parcel of how we lead. For most people, there was no conscious plan; they simply went along for the ride. Others struggled with the fundamental notion of "I got to where I am by winning, and I am not about to now start down another path and give up winning as I learned [know] that winning is a good thing." Yet it is often our winnings that prevent us from helping others to win, but by doing so, we become even smarter and stronger. It is not that people don't understand intellectually the value of shared triumphs; it is the act of creating and sharing them that presents the problem. The problem is that rationalization is a brain thing; doing is a gut thing. At the very center is (and get ready, here comes a big breakthrough idea) that people simply don't believe it because you *say* you mean them no harm. Just saying it doesn't make it so, not even if you really believe and mean it. Unless and until people are convinced that you mean them no harm, they will not accept that there are no losers in the organization. At the core of this is that you cannot simply communicate the message; you must convey it. More about this later.

I knew from the outset that writing a book would be a challenge for me. Moreover, there have been thousands of books already written about leadership. One of the things that, for me, make a big difference in how I think and approach problems is the words I choose to frame issues. It often surprises me how a single word can change one's whole way of visualizing, framing, and handling problems. One example of that is we Americans take vacations (synonyms: a break, leave, escape), whereas Europeans take holidays (synonyms: festivals, celebration, feast). Which would you rather take? How is it that changing one word can change your whole mind-set, your outlook, and your expectations? I no longer take vacations; I now take only holidays. I solved the problem of writing my book by deciding instead to write a short digest or précis. It's much simpler, with a lot less pressure. If it should end up being a book, so be it.

Let's talk about words (and the ideas behind them and the pictures they form) and their effect on our values, development, thinking, our approach to problem solving, and yes, on our concept of leadership. Let's look at the history of our industry leaders after World War II. This was the period when the unions fundamentally changed their objectives and strategies. Both my parents were union leaders. My father was a union organizer for the Teamsters union and my mother was secretary-rreasurer for the Laborers union. In the years before the war, the unions' objectives were, in my opinion, both sound and basic: to promote and protect workers' rights. After the war, the emphasis changed, and while the prewar motives were still important, restrictive work rules started to play a major role in union negotiations, and demands for ever-higher wages, seniority preference, and benefits became the rule. It was now about protecting *union* jobs (and dues) and not on growing the economy to protect the worker. Remember, back in chapter 3, we talked about a time when Walter P. Reuther, representing the UAW, asked for *both* a 30 percent increase in wages and *no* increase in the prices of GM automobiles! This, coupled with the fact that by February of 1946, the *monthly* total worker days on strike reached 23,000,000, which set the stage for a disastrous decline in manufacturing jobs that came back to haunt us in the last generation and continues to this day. The driver of this catastrophic decline is what I refer to as the union's use of the Archimedes approach to negotiating. Or the "Give me a big enough lever and I can put you out of business" strategy. You just came off a very good year. You can now expect a very tough push (the long lever approach) for higher wages and benefits. Flushed with profits, it is hard to argue against those changes, and having had a great year, management is anxious to keep the workers on the job. So the organization, in effect, gives away part of its future or, said another way, gambles that the future will be as good (predictable and profitable) as the past. So costs are ratcheted up using the lever of profits. Next year is maybe not so good, in part because of the higher wages and benefits you bargained away last year. No matter, you come out with a new line the next year, and you have another great year and another year of giveaways. However, at some point (maybe two or three decades later), you run out of new breakthroughs, or as our case is here, your costs are out of line with your new overseas competitors. The solution is to either cut back (reduce your break-even point) or start producing overseas to drive down costs. The result is a staggering loss of union (and nonunion) jobs. According to the EPI report (by Robert E. Scott, January 22, 2015), "The United States lost 5.7 million manufacturing jobs between March 1998 and 2013. The principal causes of manufacturing job losses were growing trade deficits, especially with China, Mexico, and other low-wage nations, and the weak recovery from the Great Recession since 2009." Manufacturing jobs fell from a high of almost 20 million in 1980 and drifted down to 17.5 million in 2001, when the losses declined rapidly down to about 11 million and now stands at about 12.5 million manufacturing jobs.

BLS July 15, 2015

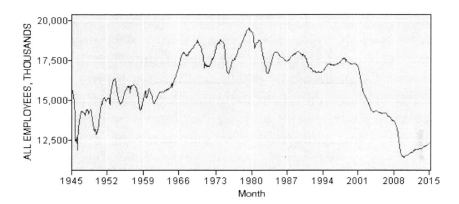

Had our leaders, both management and union alike, thought through the systemic and unintended consequences of ignoring the difference between words (and ideas) like value versus cost, profit versus profitability, fixed versus variable costs, it just might well have given the United States a strategic advantage in today's global world. But leaders were (mis)guided by their rubber bands. After all, if pay were based on the value of the work done instead of the number of years an individual has been doing the work, jobs that create a $30 per hour value (which equates to $62,400 a year) should not be paid $60 or $75 an hour simply because someone has been doing it for years. What would it take for America to regain its global competitiveness in the manufacturing sector? It may come as a surprise to some that a proposed high-speed rail line from ninety miles north of Los Angeles to San Francisco will not accomplish that objective; in fact, it won't make any difference at all. What if we could start afresh? What would it take to make our automotive industry highly competitive in this global economy? What if the price of American made cars was 10 percent or even 20 percent less than it is today? What if employees were paid based on value instead of seniority? I am *not* suggesting that seniority has no worth, but should the cost of installing a door on a car depend on how many years a person has been doing it? Let's suppose the employees were paid on value alone, and instead of endlessly leveraging up hourly wages and benefits, management and labor would agree on a fixed (once agreed to, not negotiable) percentage of *profits* to be distributed annually based primarily on seniority. This could be divided into three parts. Company-provided health benefits would be major medical only, with a $1,000 deductible. So part 1 would be a flat bonus that employees, at their discretion, could use to pay for supplemental health insurance (more benefits or lower deductible), and if they didn't feel a need for a Cadillac plan, they could use the bonus to take a holiday. Part 2 would be a bonus based entirely on seniority and weighted by job classification. Part 3 would be a retirement contribution based on a defined contribution (fixed amount in) instead of defined benefits (fixed amount out), as is now the case in many major organizations but which is being rapidly phased out in private industry. This approach would incentivize both management and union workers to focus on growth, profitability, and creating more jobs instead of on protecting union jobs. Clearly, the current approach is not working for either the organizations or their union employees. Unemployment could be a thing of the past, and we would be enjoying a vibrant and sustainable manufacturing economy. Maybe it is not too late to reinvent the wheel, so to speak. You must admit it is an intriguing idea.

Enough already. Let's get on with it. So much of leadership (especially the teaching part) focuses on matters like vision, motivation, strategy, communication, risk taking, innovation, and charisma, and so on and so on. I think this is why is it so hard to bring out the natural leadership in individuals, because its basis is that of layering on (or adding) those characteristics in common with other successful leaders. This does nothing to address the need to unlearn the behaviors that make these candidates in need of leadership training in the first place. I think leadership has much more to do with *why* we do what we do and less to do with what it is we do. Not to say that what we do is unimportant, but giving someone a fish feeds them for a day, while teaching them to fish feeds them for life. We need to rethink the "Give them a fish" training strategy and look beyond what it is leaders need to do and what they need to do consistently, day after day, week after week, year after year.

Let's revisit our youth. We all know what zero-sum is. We learned that if there is a winner, there *must* be a loser. This is how we were raised. After all, we learned in high school that it is a matter of physics. As Newton's third law of reciprocal actions postulates, "All forces occur in pairs, and these two forces are equal in magnitude and opposite in direction." It is this notion of "equal but opposite" that has us thinking that Newton's third law applies just as well to human behavior as it does to physics. For much of our life that is, in fact, just how it works out. If I win, you lose, or vice versa. It is this duality that hampers and diminishes our effectiveness as leaders, notwithstanding its success in certain limited situations. Where we need to begin is at the beginning and not in the middle. Let's look at some everyday non-zero-sum examples to see how they differ from the zero-sum experiences we had in our own everyday lives. First let me make this distinction clear. I am not talking about win-win negotiations. While negotiating and leadership have some common characteristics (i.e., behaviors), they are entirely different things. Moreover, I disagree with those who propose that in negotiations, you should always go for the win-win solution. The win-win approach assumes you care about maintaining the relationship, which is not always the case. If you are negotiating with your spouse or your children, I sincerely hope you care a great deal about the long-term relationship. If you are negotiating with a supplier or a staff member, I would assume you care about the relationship. On the other hand, if you are negotiating with someone to paint your family room, you may or may not care about a long-term relationship. So how you approach one versus the other may well be quite different depending on the circumstances. You may not care about finding a win-win solution with your house painter. However, *leadership* is all about building long-term relationships with those you care about and count on, starting with integrity and building on trust. I am not suggesting that if you have integrity and are trusted you will be successful as a leader. What I am saying is that without these qualities, there is precious little chance you will ever be an effective leader. In the final analysis, I like to think one overriding principle of leadership should be to *leave no losers behind*. Unfortunately, zero-sum leaders usually leave a lot of casualties lying around bleeding. So let's take a look at a typical non-zero-sum (in this case a win-win) situation in which there are no losers. Say you have just bought a car. You feel like a winner because you (presumably) got the deal you wanted or you would not have purchased the car. What you have just concluded is the classic non-zero-sum game. The dealership sold you the car (only) because they valued the money you agreed to pay more than the car they just sold you. You, on the other hand, valued the car more than the money you just agreed to pay. In this situation, there are no losers. You both got what you most valued, and thus it is a non-zero-sum outcome. It is what you do every day in a grocery store when you buy a quart of milk. You agree to pay a price for the milk because you think the milk is worth more to you than the money you agreed to pay (otherwise you would go elsewhere or not buy the milk), and the grocer thinks the amount you have agreed to pay is worth more to the store than the quart of milk, and thus you agree to a non-zero-sum exchange. There are no losers in this transaction. You can think of this as a win-win, and it is, but there is more to it than just that. All win-win outcomes are non-zero-sum, but not all non-zero-sum outcomes are win-win.

One company I worked for, which had a long history of giving Christmas bonuses to all its employees, had a particularly bad year and decided not to give out bonuses that year. It could be expected that this would create a hardship on some employees as they, no doubt, had already spent the money on gifts or were counting on it for that purpose. The vice president and treasurer had decided not to tell the employees but simply not pay the bonus. I felt this was unacceptable. People don't like getting bad news, but rather that than being put in what could be a financial bind. This was the same vice president I was unsuccessful (chapter 8) in convincing not to reprimand the director of IT. Never to be daunted by my past failures, I gave it another go. I asked if I could tell just one person (I didn't mention any particular person) that there would be no Christmas bonuses that year. He found it hard to argue that I could not tell even a single person, and fortunately, he never asked who that person would be. Armed with his approval, I immediately went to the *right* person in the organization, and by the end of the day, everybody knew there would be no bonuses that year. As far as the treasurer knew, he was still a winner, but the company, in my opinion, rescued a lot of people who otherwise would have been losers. Clearly the employees were not winners, but they were not losers.

Non-zero-sum leadership is really about relationships and interactions that result in increased worth (or value) to both parties but, at the very least, add worth to one without losses to the other. I can remember, as a young boy, that the cartons of milk always had some lesson printed on them. One that has stuck with me all these years (a takeoff from a poem that predates the Mayflower called "The Optimists Creed" ["The optimist the doughnut sees; the pessimist the hole"]) is apropos to our discussion here of non-zero-sum leadership, and that is "as you ramble on through life, keep our eye upon the donut and not upon the hole." Focusing on the hole is often mistaken for progress, and it sinks many leaders. The non-zero-sum leader sees things differently and never loses sight of the objective, i.e., the donut. Once I was offered the job of reorganizing virtually all the administrative functions (from sales to accounting to production to IT) of a large food-processing company, and the president asked me what I wanted "to be vice president of." A bell went off, and whistles started to blow; this was the goal I had set for myself fifteen years ago—to be a senior executive in a major corporation before I was forty! Even though this would have put me five years ahead of my plan, I turned it down. The president asked why I didn't want to be a vice president, and I replied, "Given what you have asked me to do, no matter what you put after the words *vice president of*, people would know what I'm *not* supposed to do." My focus was on the doughnut, and while the hole was very tempting, the doughnut was the more convincing. (I suggested simply a title of *internal consultant*.)

Chapter Seven

The Starting Blocks

> Until one is committed, there is hesitancy, the chance to draw back, always ineffectiveness. Concerning all acts of initiative and creation, there is one elementary truth the ignorance of which kills countless ideas and splendid plans: that the moment one definitely commits oneself, and then providence moves too. Whatever you can do, begin it. Boldness has genius, power and magic in it. Begin it now.
>
> —Johann Wolfgang von Goethe

Of all the qualities that characterize a good (or great) leader, the single most important one that must be present is *passion*. All the other qualities, absent passion, will amount to little. Not that passion is enough, but it is the starting block on which all the others rest, and it powers all the rest. There are people thrust (or

dragged) into leadership roles that are competent but not passion-ate. Passionate people can accomplish great things; competent people (absent passion) make good administrators but not great leaders. I challenge you to think of one great leader (whether for good or evil) that was (or is) not passionate.

Along with passion comes purpose, they are two peas in a pod. It is not possible to be passionate about nothing. Whether it is to build a better something, rid the world of pain and suffering, cre-ate a world-class company, save souls, or win a gold medal at the Olympics, the two *P*s go hand in hand. However, when it comes to passion and purpose, environmental factors can play a major part. While passion and purpose have a genetic component, it is not the sole determinant. More often than not, you either have these qual-ities or you don't, but in some few instances, a life-changing expe-rience, a death in the family, a rebirth, a major medical trauma, or some such factor can trigger your deepest passions and set you on a new life course.

But let's step back a bit and put our journey into perspective. To better understand the mind-set and its effect on our passion that took us to this place in time, let's try our hands at some amateur forensic cultural anthropology. Anthropologists use the term *culture* to refer to a society or group in which many or all people live and think in similar ways. It has several distinguishing characteristics. A people's culture includes their beliefs, rules of behavior, rituals, styles of dress, ways of producing and cooking food, as well as their political and economic systems. It is based on *symbols*—abstract ways of referring to and understanding ideas, objects, feelings, or behaviors—and the ability to communicate symbols using language. People in the same society tend to share common behaviors and ways of thinking. While people biologically inherit many physical traits and behavioral instincts, culture is learned and socially inherited. A person must learn culture from other people in a society. I realize that any analysis of this sort will come up short, but that is the nature of culture. Any descriptive commentary will, by default, tend to over-simplify and generalize. Not everyone in any particular society (or country) will behave the same or cook the same foods or dress alike,

but there is a tendency toward that and ever more so with the ubiqui-
tous status of communications technology. If we start by looking first
at the typical American upbringing, starting in the forties, we should
remember that those who fought in WWII were children born (or
raised) during the Depression era. The values we might expect from
that generation would include having one parent holding a (single)
good job—for life—and the other raising the children and laying the
foundation for building a family. We would expect an inclination
toward not wanting to upset the applecart, to fit in, not rock the
boat, and to get along. These values would have been reinforced by
military service. Coming, as these individuals did, from a generation
that had neither the resources nor the will to spend beyond their limited means, it is not too surprising that we saw a focus on going to
college (by the tens of thousands), starting families, settling in, and
enjoying a certain amount of economic freedom. Not unpredictably,
there was an increase in birth rates from 19/1,000 in 1940 to over
25/1,000 between 1952 and 1957. The birth rate hit a high in 1954
(coincidently, the same year that America first introduced bucket
seats in production automobiles, making the long-established practice of snuggling a thing of the past), following soon thereafter the
decline of drive-in theaters, which hit their peak in the late fifties and
early sixties, small wonder that the birth rates steadily dropped, now
stuck at some 14/1,000. Just after the war, the U.S. GDP was some
$39 billion. That increased in the next decade by 90 percent and the
next by 75 percent, and then between 1966 and 1976, it jumped to
123 percent, and in the decade between 1976 and 1986, it jumped
by an incredible 158 percent, dropping the next decade to 89 percent, and then, in the most recent ten-year period (ending in 2006),
the rate of growth was only 51 percent. Do you think it is possible
that the bloom is off the rose? What is made clear by these numbers
is the fact that beginning after the war, the economy gradually built
up a head of steam until the boiler blew in 1986. Those who took
us through the first three decades after the war did so with the wind
behind them. It was, during this period, almost impossible to make
a mistake, and everything looked up. The rubber band approach was
working! In part, this growth was a function not just of birth rates

but of how this new generation of parents raised their children. This was the age of indulgence. Those who fought the war now found that they could provide for their children in ways their parents could not for them, and they did so with a reckless abandon.

While in their parents' generation college was the exception, it now became the rule. Now the push is for everyone to have a college education. The reality is, however, that not all are cut out for the rigors of an academic education. We live under the assumption that anyone that graduates from high school is suited for college, when in fact, the average IQ in the United States is 98. As for our global educational relative competitiveness measured against students in places like Hong Kong (IQ averages 107), South Korea (IQ averages 106), and Japan (IQ averages 105), they are better suited (based on readiness for the challenges for academic life) than U.S. students. Even Dr. Peter Drucker once remarked that we are an "overeducated" society and what we needed were more plumbers and mechanics.

There is a tendency to measure our personal competitiveness against those we see around us and not those in other countries. My child got an A in math, but Bobby only got a B, so my child is "ready" to take on the challenges of the world, and besides, my kid wore designer jeans. Why not a car for graduation from high school, surely that would mean they will succeed in college? I am not judging any of this but simply pointing out that the generation that got us here did so with the burden of the Depression in terms of childhood values and expectations, but early on, that generation was confronted with a very different set of realities and was not really well prepared for the new expectations and responsibilities of this new world. The worldview of these individuals was very different from that which now greets us every morning. The youngest generation of managers now entering the workforce does so with a very different set of values, expectations, and self-confidence, not always justified. The good news was that with the seemingly ever-expanding economy that greeted the children of the Depression era came opportunities to take risks. Those with passion took risks, and things kept going up and up, and as it did so, more people of passion took even greater risks. I am reminded of the Xerox story. When xerography was first invented, the president of the company had three independent studies made of the technology's market potential and its possible applications. All three (including one conducted internally) came to the same conclusion. "Why would people need to make copies when they already have carbon paper?" The president of Xerox decided to move ahead anyway. Opportunities were everywhere to be had for those with vision and courage.

I still think the best example of just how unprepared the United States is for this new world is that, until very recently, when one took up another language, we in America called it a foreign language, whereas other counties have always referred to them as a second or third language. Everything and everybody else were seen as foreign. We thought of ourselves not as simply exceptional but as standing apart and unconnected to the rest of the world. Yes, they bought our products and services and we bought their's, but it had little impact or influence on our daily lives. Most of our actions were predicated on *our* worldview, and little attention was paid to those activities going on elsewhere.

Global competition in those days meant America decided to sell its products or services abroad. This mind-set worked just fine for a long time, and it is what, ultimately, set the stage for our global erosion. It is not yet an implosion, although we have lost major industries that will never be recovered or replaced. Indeed, if you think hard about it, the only things that can't be outsourced or offshored are things we need to reach out and touch—like hamburgers, plumbers, and house painters.

Of course, this "Nothing can go wrong" attitude was fortified during the one-thousand-day cost-and-price freeze, which effectively solidified the notion that labor costs could be allowed to rise without any fundamental damage to the economy and certainly not from competition abroad. This now seems to be the case with federal deficits, which, I suspect, will have much the same outcome: a massive failure of the economy. Bear in mind that "the only difference between a recession and a Depression is that in the former you are unemployed, in that latter I am unemployed."

73

The factors that will take us to this seemingly unavoidable end are already upon us, but no one seems to take notice or apparently even care. Everyone knows that the population distribution is shifting and that there is a growing percent that is over the age of sixty-five. In 1950, that was 8.1 percent of the total, in 1975 it was 10.5 percent, and in 2000, it was 12.4 percent, and by 2015, it expected to reach 18.2 percent. There is, however, another important factor that has not been, that I have seen, factored in this, and that is the much smaller wages earned by the fastest-growing segment of the working population—the hospitality or service industry. At present, there are some twenty-one million employed in goods production and fifty-six million employed in the food and hospitality industry. With the average wage in the service sector of about one-half to one-third of that in the goods-producing sector, the FICA burden (not just paid by fewer people but people in much-lower-paying jobs) will bankrupt the system, if not the country. This could have been solved twenty, fifteen, or even ten years ago, but now the alternatives are to double the FICA and/or raise the retirement age to seventy or seventy-five. In addition, the rapid growth of the budget deficit will result in a crushing tax burden and inflation rates not seen since the Carter administration, paid for by future generations.

What has all this to do with leadership? I believe that it will take people of great passion, clear purpose, an ability to think strategically, and boundless courage to steer us clear of the shoals. Not just our organizations but our country is at risk. We now have the highest corporate tax rates in the world, and businesses are already starting to move to other, more business friendly countries. It will take those with a long view and a commitment to keeping America strong. Can non-zero-sum leadership make any real difference? I believe that focusing on the core values of non-zero-sum leadership—integrity, trust, courage, risk taking, and innovation—can make a difference. It is important, however, to understand that yesterday's solutions cannot undo the damage. Passion and purpose are necessary and are capable of producing great outcomes but, by themselves, are not sufficient. It will take business leaders of vision that equals their passion and purpose to make America once again the light that burned so brightly.

When it comes to cutting through to the fundamental core issues, I am reminded of Dr. Russell Ackoff's insightful observations when serving in the U.S. Army in the Philippines during WWII. A study was conducted to determine where additional protection should be added to increase the survival rate of bombers. After the study group made its presentation (augmented with ample data), Dr. Ackoff put one question to the group, "But didn't you study the planes that came back?"

CHAPTER EIGHT

Integrity, Unlike a GPS, Is Not an Option

Integrity is the essence of everything successful.

—Richard Buckminster Fuller

There are almost a dozen qualities that, I believe, leaders must possess to be successful in our culture. Not all are of equal import, and it is possible to be a leader without all of them. For example, *integrity* is critical to leadership in most but not all cultures. It is therefore possible to be a leader in some cultures and still lack integrity. I place, in our culture, it as second only to *passion* or *purpose*. The two *P*s will get you so far, but if you lack integrity, you will eventually fail. We are talking about responsibility, morals, trust and trusting, and truth telling as part and parcel of integrity. You may get away without these qualities, even for a long time, but in our society, you will sooner or later be exposed.

Dr. David Berlo and I were together one evening some years ago having a glass of wine and some great conversation. He was a very perceptive (not to mention profound) person, and he shared another of his many interesting and powerful insights with me. He said that one "should never promise to *always* tell the truth, but rather never to lie." The distinction being that truth telling is about facts, and as one cannot always (almost never for that matter) know *all* the facts, it is usually not possible to always tell the truth as truth is a function of *content*. On the other hand, lying is a matter of *intent*.

With this thought in mind, we come to the next most important characteristic of the non-zero-sum leader. As Ralph Waldo Emerson said, "Nothing is at last sacred but the integrity of your own mind." As the legend (myth?) goes, Washington's father said (after being told by George that he had cut down the cherry tree), "My son, that you should not be afraid to tell the truth as it is more to me than a thousand trees! Yes, though they were blossomed with silver and had leaves of the purest gold!"

Integrity is not something you put on in the morning to look good at the office and then take off and hang up when you go home in the evening. Integrity is not what you do just when it favors you but what you do when it favors others as well. It is taking the time to explain to the store clerk who tries to give you a refund at the full regular price for something you bought yesterday at the sale price but are now returning. It is correcting the waiter when he forgot to charge you for the dessert you had, or pointing out to the cab driver that he gave you too much change.

This journey is about who we are, reflecting on how we got to be who we are and reexamining the programming that is now part and parcel of how we lead. For many, there was no conscious plan; they simply went with the flow. Others struggled with the fundamental issue of "I got to where I am by winning, and I am not about to give that edge away, and certainly not freely." Yet it is sometimes our very successes that fail us, for it is through our failures that we (should) become smarter and stronger. It is not that people don't understand intellectually the value of shared triumphs; it is the doing that causes the predicament. Unless and until people are convinced that you mean them no harm, they will not accept that there are no losers in the organization. I have since expanded Dr. Berlo's concept to include the idea that people must not only know that you mean them no harm but that you mean them well. At the core of this is that you cannot communicate the message; you must convey it.

Early in my career, I had the opportunity to build from the ground up a management information system for a large food-processing company. In the process of hiring the team, a woman applied for one of the positions for which she was well qualified. One of the questions on the employment application was the person's salary requirement. Her's was on the low side, and so when I later offered her the position, the salary I offered was higher than she had asked for. Some would ask, "Why would you do that?" First, it was the right thing to do, and second, she knew from that point on the company meant her no harm and could be counted on to treat her fairly. Just as importantly, I suspect, as a result, that those around her may have been influenced by her experience.

Let me give you another example of finding an "I mean you no harm" non-zero-sum solution and its contribution to creating a nonloser culture. Some years ago, I ran an IT department that came to me with some inherited and very serious quality and credibility problems. One major problem was that someone in the data entry section was leaking payroll information even before the department managers had the opportunity to discuss the payroll changes with their employees. This was, understandably, causing major concerns within the company, and it had to be fixed and quickly. As it turned out, it was common knowledge who the leakee was, and so the simple (zero-sum) solution would be not to let that individual process payroll information or (better still, some have argued) to terminate the employee. However, another major problem that also needed addressing was that this department had, as you might imagine, low self-esteem as the department was often the subject of watercooler jokes and worse. Either of the two solutions above would have exacerbated an already serious morale problem. What was needed was a solution that would be a first step in the rebuilding process. What was actually done in this case was to restrict the entry of payroll information to only three people in the data entry section instead of the past practice of distributing it to whoever was available or willing. The list of the three who were authorized to enter this sensitive information was posted on the department bulletin board for the entire department (and anyone else who came through the main door) to see. The person who was leaking the information was one of the three on the list. We never again had a problem, and no bodies were left on the floor. "I mean you no harm" is about finding solutions that build up, not tear down. An important part of the buildup is inclusion. If people don't feel a part of the organization, it will result in not just underperformance but also underachieving. You will leave potentials untapped and aspirations unmet. Let me share two examples of how one might bring about inclusion. The president had decided to conduct an employee survey. He had hired a company to meet with the top three dozen or so managers to construct a profile. I thought we were missing a great opportunity to create a feeling of inclusion, and I suggested that he include in the announcement that *any* employee not scheduled for an interview who wished to be included to just let us know. Now, I was pretty sure no one would take us up on that offer, and no one did, but imagine the difference in how they felt about the company and its offer. Another example was the lunch meeting with my entire staff of 120 at the Hyatt. I also invited the president, executive vice president, and all the senior vice presidents to attend, and they all did. The purpose of this meeting was to have each of my senior staff give a short presentation, starting with what their job was. After all, how many people know what the corporate treasurer does? I also asked that they each lay out their plans for the coming year. There was a little hesitation on the part of the IT department as they were planning to reorganize and reduce the staff. I told him to tell it like it is. On the way back to the office in the elevator, a secretary (I suppose many of you don't know what that is either) thanked me and said that it was the first time anyone had ever taken the time to explain just how the organization fits together and how her function related to the other parts that made up the finance department. I like to think that same sense of inclusion was shared by others.

While reaching the "I mean you no harm" state is crucial to becoming a non-zero-sum leader, it is no simple matter, and there are some significant obstacles to overcome. The winning and losing notion is deep-seated in both our psyche and our culture, and changing that attitude takes vision, courage, and persistence. If we are ever to fundamentally change this disconnect between people and organizations and achieve meaningful and sustainable change in organizational performance without constant turmoil and the all-too-frequent displacement of jobs, there is no alternative. The challenge is, however, enormous. One example of just how high that bar has been set is the interview some years ago with ten CEOs of major organizations, where one of the questions asked was, "What was the toughest decision you ever made?"

Nine of the ten replied, "Letting those [thousands] of people go." I understand that once you are there, you may have few options, but was it possible to end up at another there? Certainly, in today's global economy, the pressure is enormous. That plus the fact that the markets have precious little patient money (stock markets will give you, at most, ninety days). This leaves little room or forgiveness for more gradual and less disruptive change. This lack of a long view by the markets is precisely why some organizations prefer to stay private: it gives them the luxury of focusing on the long-term outcomes and not just the short-term profits. Toyota is a good (if rare) example of a public company taking this long view approach. Very early in its move to expand its market to the United States, it set its prices at a level that *assumed* their factories were running at full capacity, even though they were not. The underlying strategic consideration was that if they priced them in this way (forgoing profits in the short run), eventually their factories would be at full capacity. You can decide for yourself if that gave them a sustainable competitive advantage. Sometimes perhaps it is the road less traveled that takes us to the next big opportunity. Still, not all this pressure is bad. It has kept America the most productive country in the world and has afforded us, so far, a standard of living unmatched by any other country.

Since there is little chance this global trend and its attendant pressures will slow anytime in the near future, it argues for fundamental changes in the way we lead organizations, as that may offer the single best strategic alternative to these periodic and painful midcourse corrections. How can this be realized in a practical way? In the process of reorganizing the major functions of one of the companies I worked for, it happened that, over the years, they had taken on some functions that were, at best, marginally contributing to the organization's short-term viability and undercutting its long-term success. At this point, the problem was one of preventing the failure of the company. In the reorganization process, some departments, of necessity, were eliminated. The first step was to create the space to reorganize and refocus its human assets. However, there were individuals in these areas and departments that had a great deal to offer this company, and these would prove invaluable to the rebuilding process. These individuals were grouped into something named the *corporate staff*. This was a staff like no other. To start, I asked for and got a commitment from the president that the staff would never write reports. Where the organization had a problem, a team from the staff would analyze the problem, come up with a solution, *and* implement it. The staff would work under the functional head but report indirectly to me. The functional head and I consulted on many issues, including raises. A key to its success (and it was *very* successful) was that I knew the aspirations of the staff members. I knew what they wanted from their careers at this company, and I took advantage of that knowledge in putting together the teams and matching *their* goals to the challenge. In some instances, they took on important management positions that, had they been hired from the outside, would have paid them considerably more than the salary they made as corporate staff members. Not once did anyone ever ask for more money. They were on track to reach their professional goals and to making a real difference in the process. What a wonderful period in my life (and I hope theirs). The changes that were brought about were so successful that within three years, the company had a bottom line that exceeded the combined profits of the prior fifteen years.

CHAPTER NINE

Where the Rubber Meets the Road

> Vision must be followed by the venture. It is not
> enough to stare up the steps—we must step up
> the stairs.
>
> —Vance Havner

If we are to successfully lay one block upon another, we need to seriously rethink our long-held notions of control as they are inextricably linked with our concepts regarding vision, focus, foresight, and ultimately, performance.

It is one thing to have a vision but quite another to rally others around it and to plan for its successful execution. All too often, we may have a vision, but without focus and authenticity, you can wander around the desert forever. The non-zero-sum leader starts by understanding that challenges will arise and so sees the need to focus more on *outcomes* and less on *process*, as that is what gives the vision its focus. Forget the hole and concentrate on the doughnut. Understanding that organizations were *invented* to solve problems prepares you for the journey. Moses would not have needed to organize the exodus if he knew there would never be any problems. Indeed, I think most people go into management precisely because they like solving problems—at least those people who become successful.

A small example of how this plays out in organizations: I needed a mechanical engineer on the corporate staff. The organization had some issues in the production area that required the skills of such a person. Since the plan was to eventually transfer this individual to the senior vice president of production after the project was completed, I thought it best to have the senior vice president interview him also. After the two of them had spent some time together, I met with the senior vice president and asked what he thought. He said he would not hire him, and of course, I wanted to know why. I should tell you that one of the things I liked about this particular candidate was that he complemented the senior vice president by bringing to the table some skills that were needed in the production department. The reason the senior vice president did not want to hire him was basically that the applicant's strengths were the senior vice president's weaknesses, and he didn't see the need for him. I hired the applicant. But now I was armed with all the reasons the senior vice president would not hire him, so we had a long and detailed discussion about what were seen as issues by the senior vice president so that the applicant could know what "right" would look like. To succeed in any organization (or for that matter, in life), you need to know what to aim for. Zero-sum leaders tend to operate on the presumption that people should somehow *know* what to do and when they make a mistake (and only then) do they find out what was expected of them. In a non-zero-sum world, the notion of control looks very different from that of a zero-sum world. It no longer means power, rule, restrain, monitor, manipulate, or limit. It now means to be able to forecast outcomes with predictable certainty. In order to do that with a high degree of consistency, one must start with defining the vision and getting agreement on what success would look like. All too often, leaders think professionals should *know* what doing the right job looks like without any involvement (or effort) on the part of the leader. Many of us were raised in an environment where the norm was telling people what they did wrong rather than telling them what right would have looked like. Sound familiar? This is leadership by a slap on the back of the head, not unlike that T-shirt I saw on a small child that said, "My Name Is Not No No No." Too many leaders would rather let people try to figure it out on their own; that way, the leader is in control. The non-zero-sum leader takes the time to communicate to people what right would look like and then help them get there.

As Robert Collier said, "Vision reaches beyond the thing that is, into the conception of what can be. Imagination gives you the picture. Vision gives you the impulse to make the picture your own." The objective (vision) in rebuilding the IT department was to construct a department that thought of themselves as among the best. Of course, non-zero-sum leadership is based on the conviction that people want to do well and, whenever possible, make a difference. Are we sometimes disappointed? Of course, but to go through life operating on the assumption that people don't want to do good work makes your life (and theirs) miserable, and most often, you get exactly what you expect of them. Let's use another example from that same IT department. The level of data entry output was well below what was both necessary and possible. In a zero-sum world, one first looks at all the controls that could be put in place to increase productivity, and there are plenty of schemes for that sort of thing. The problem with all these controls is someone has to control the controls. That is, constantly monitor performance and correct (i.e., provide training, cajole, reprimand, or fire) any underperformers. That takes time and resources, and its foundation is based on the premise that people need to be constantly managed to perform good work. Another solution involved using a creditable measure of *overall* performance (based on output) and creating a weekly chart to post on the department bulletin board. It was *not* posted by individual but reflected only the performance for the data entry department *as a whole*. That was *all* that was done. No operator was ever called in for counseling, no additional training was undertaken, and no one was ever fired. Yet somehow, each week, the performance chart gradually started (seemingly magically) to show improvement, and within a few months, the output had increased by almost 50 percent.

Let's look at another example, this one from a major food processor. The plant productivity and cost controls were based on a hypothetical basic case of canned product. For canned peaches (let's say), that might be a 303 can size, fancy fruit, and with heavy sugar. There would be a standard cost to produce that product, and then every can of peaches (whatever can size and whatever amount of sugar was added or grade of fruit in the can) would be converted by using ratios to make it "equal" to a 303, and if the fruit was not fancy, a ratio would be applied to "adjust" for the quality of the fruit and yet another if they were not packed in heavy sugar. To start with this is a convoluted approach and, at best, became a very rough (and totally useless) approximation. Worse still was that fact that what the plant managers got was a dollar figure that simply said the standard basic case cost $x.xx and your costs were plus or minus $x.xx. Ask yourself what you would do with such information. At best, it is frustrating (even potentially harmful) information because managers *don't* manage costs, at least not directly. Whoa, you say, of course they are responsible for costs. I agree, but they don't (and can't) manage costs. What they can manage (and control) is people, product, and productivity, which, of course, translates into costs. So out went the industry standard basic case and in came an entirely new system. Using computer regression techniques, we were able to set industrial engineered standards for about 96 percent of all the operations and products in the processing plant. Lacking enough data to come up with standards for the last 4 percent, we simply asked the plant managers for their estimates. Remember, I said, non-zero-sum leadership is based on the conviction that people want to do well. By asking the plant managers, it not only got us to 100 percent but accomplished something else, and that was that they had a piece of the decision and that gave them a sense of confidence and a stake in what we were doing. Now each function had standard hours by function, product, can size, sugar, etc., so we had the data needed to feed the managers information based on what they actually managed. They could now see that the standard called for four peach sorters on the swing shift, and the manager had five. Now that is information they can do something with. But we didn't stop there. It doesn't do a lot of good (for anyone) to tell you tomorrow what you should have done differently yesterday. That is classic zero-sum leadership by no no no. Now the difference between a model and a system is that accounting *systems* typically work in only *one* direction: they collect data and regurgitate the numbers. On the other hand, a *model* works in both directions. Since we had the standards necessary to collect and calculate, it was not a major leap to precalculate and predict. In other words, the plant managers could now input their production plans for tomorrow, and the computer would tell them how to staff the plant, how many people, on which jobs, and on which of the three shifts. I have oversimplified for purposes of clarity, but as there were union contracts involved that set wages based on hours worked in each job, the model had to consider those constraints when making staffing recommendations. Yes, it actually *told* the plant manager *who* to put on each job to minimize the costs and optimize production. Hold on, you say, I don't care what the computer tells me. I want Mike on that forklift. The model permitted the plant managers to override the system to allow for preferences based on factors not known to the computer. One other important change (which we will talk about in chapter 13) was that instead of getting the reports at the end of the next day's production, they now got them at the beginning of the next day instead of the end, but that is a story for later in the book.

But then as a former CFO, I firmly believe that organizations should have not one but three accounting systems. One is needed to meet the organization's fiduciary obligation, which is the least demanding in terms of accuracy. I know that much is made about accuracy in accounting, but in point of fact, this information is designed for C-Suite folks, banks, and the investors, and what they really care about is not whether product A should get a $.00018 overhead allocation of rent or a $.00024 allocation for energy. What they want, and need, is to make sure that all the costs that went into the bucket come out of the bucket and do it without deception and in a consistent way. Said another way, it doesn't make a lot of difference to the game if the goal posts are 100 yards apart or 110 yards so long as they are the same for each game.

The second function of accounting should be to provide information to managers in terms of what it is they actually can and do manage, and except for the financial staff, few operating units, if any, manage by the numbers. I understand that all these operating units have budgets and that they are judged by how well they meet those numbers. One thing I insisted upon was if a business unit was presented with an important opportunity to undertake something unplanned at budget time that they come to me to discuss it. No opportunity should slip through our hands because some unit did not plan for it or have the budget for it. Budgets are a quantification of a plan, and while I would argue that planning is important, the facts sometimes change.

System number 3 is a strategic cost-accounting system. This system is, in effect, ad hoc. That is, when a decision is needed to add a product, drop a product, enter a new market, open a new distribution center, or the like, at that point, what an organization needs is a one-off analysis of the costs and benefits of such a move. All too often, such decisions are made using standard accounting methods. If you are thinking about dropping a product, will it actually reduce your insurance or your rent or your cost of capital? Strip away all these indirect allocations to get at the real costs of the proposal and look at the decision from a strategic cost point of view. How this plays out is yet another example for this same company. Asked to put together a short-range plan, I undertook a study of the various products and their profitability. Note that I said profitability and not profits as profitability is an operating term whereas profit is an accounting term. This company was still using the old basic case approach, and by doing some reverse engineering, I was immediately drawn to one particular product: choice-grade apricots. The accounting system told me that the cost to produce this item was only $0.10 more per case, and it sold for $0.50 more. On the surface, this item was a real winner. I was drawn to this item because the company produced only nine hundred cases of this product. At $0.10 per case, that meant that the total added cost to produce this product versuss allowing it to simply flow into the irregular (rather than picking out the choice pieces) was only $900. Having spent time earlier in my career as a senior industrial engineer, that just did not make any sense to me. I walked over to the plant and asked to see the line that produced that product. The season is some six weeks long; the sorting line (needed *only* to pick out the choice fruit from the irregular) has eight sorters. The line runs twenty-four hours a day for the full product cycle, and all it costs is $900? You can immediately see a new course of action here once you strip away the standard cost accounting system.

A recently published interview with a CFO in a major organization makes the argument for me. The organization is buying back billions of dollars in their own stock because that has (according to the CFO) the best rate of return. Incidentally, this was a major drug firm where, in my view, buying back your own stock translates into no pipeline of new drugs. Organizations also need not one but three rates of returns. First is the zero rate of return. Meeting regulatory requirements does not require passing a rate of return test. To undertake a project that is critical to maintaining a market or strategic leadership position should have a lower (perhaps even much lower) decision threshold than undertaking new major projects that are important for long-term growth, competitiveness, and/or profitability of the organization.

Since we started this chapter with the link between control and vision, let's end this chapter with a classic example of a zero-sum approach to control and its impact on vision, growth, and morale. Many years ago, having been recently promoted to assistant to the president, I had a meeting to attend in San Francisco, a day's trip there and back. After my promotion, I had recommended one of the staff to take my place as director of management systems (now known as IT). As it happened, he also needed to go into the city and asked if he could ride along with me. I said yes but suggested he check it out with his boss, the vice president and treasurer. The vice president could not be found, and so he came along without permission. The next morning, the vice president asked why I had taken the IT manager to the city with me, and I explained what had occurred. He decided that he needed to call in the new IT manager and, in effect, reprimand him for making that decision without consulting him. I tried to explain that, in my opinion, this is exactly the wrong thing to do. As the individual was now in control of all the company's information systems, the one thing you want (need) of him is that he be able to make independent decisions. Telling him that he should not (i.e., could not be trusted to) make even such a trivial decision as going into the city on his own would do exactly the opposite of what was needed. One wants to lay the stones one upon the other (to build confidence) rather than tear down the stones. My suggestion was to decide if this was a truly critical mistake and a punishable offense. If not, let it go. If it was a minor infraction and if they continued to occur and came to represent a pattern of behavior, then a talk might be productive. If, on the other hand, this was a major breach of protocol, then, by all means, give him a verbal thrashing. The point being that, in this situation, one wants to do those things that create winners and not losers. The vision here should be to build his decision-making strengths and not tear them down. This is clearly not a no no no situation. It is interesting and sometimes even useful to reverse our thinking and to examine the possible outcomes. There were several programmers in the department, but one, while a good programmer, was the world's worst tester. If the program didn't blow up, he was satisfied even if it did not produce the desired outcomes. Talking did no good, so I put him in charge of testing all (not just his) programs before releasing them into production. Think that solved the problem?

CHAPTER TEN

The Art of Influencing Others (AKA Charisma)

> He has a way of moving and a charisma. When he steps on the ice, he has an aura about him that many people never achieve.
>
> —Frank Carroll

Some management experts believe that charisma should be at the top of the leadership list. They make the argument that without it, you cannot and will not become a great leader, perhaps even a leader at all. I agree with their "without it" premise, but I also believe that charisma at the top of the list is a recipe for disaster as it clears the way for leaders that lack *integrity*. As Ralph Archbold said, "Charisma is the transference of enthusiasm." Jim Jones and Charles Manson had charisma but not integrity. They had passion and purpose but not integrity. Theodore Roosevelt and John Kennedy had charisma, as did Ronald Regan. So did Hitler and Stalin, but there is a clear difference when one mobilizes for good versus evil, and what separates the wheat from the chaff is called purpose and integrity.

The concept of charisma is biblical and is originally defined as a divinely conferred gift or power, as a spiritual power or personal quality that gives an individual influence or authority over large numbers of people, as the special virtue of an office, function, position, etc., that confers or is thought to confer on the person the concept of charisma as a personality trait. Archbold mentioned several types of worldwide charismatic leaders, and the term began to acquire a life of its own. Weber went on to say that "the recognition on the part of those subject to authority" is decisive for the validity of charisma. In other words, while charisma is an unusual ability for leadership, it is only valuable if believers recognize such charisma in those they therefore treat as leaders. Today, leaders, government officials, prominent religious officials, and sometimes ordinary individuals are often described as charismatic. Charismatic leaders stand up usually in times of crisis, in which the basic values, the foundation of institutions, and the legitimacy of the organization are questioned. An extraordinary situation calls forth a charismatic authority structure so that charisma, at least temporarily, leads to actions, movements, and events outside the sphere of everyday life. Charisma rejects or transcends routine life. Charisma deals with the existing, the self-evident, and the established order. It works like a catalyst in an organization. Weber also said that there are three types of charisma. Charismatic authority is one of three forms of authority, the other two being traditional (feudal) authority and legal, or rational, authority. A somewhat different position was taken by Pierre Bourdieu, who argued that charisma usually depended on an "inaugural act," such as a decisive battle or moving speech, after which the charismatic person will be regarded as such. But it was Ralph Waldo Emerson in 1850 who warned "Beware of charisma" when he made his famous comment about the great men in a democracy. "Is there some common quality among these Representative Men who have been most successful as our leaders? I call it the need to be authentic—or, as our dictionaries tell us, *conforming to fact and therefore worthy of trust, reliance or belief.* While the charismatic has an uncanny outside source of strength, the authentic is strong because he is what he seems to be." If charisma is a necessary component of leadership, can it be taught? There are some who think so. I am not entirely convinced that *charisma* per se can be taught, as one can possess it only if others believe it to be so. However, at the core, it is the art of influence. Leaders that are considered charismatic leaders tend to have similar basic characteristics such as communications and rhetorical skills, expert power, self-confidence, and self-assurance; they are assertive, dynamic, outgoing, forceful, and exhibit a need for power with low authoritarianism. As Bernard M. Bass said in 1985, "Charisma is in the eye of the beholder and, therefore, is relative to the beholder. Nevertheless, the charismatic leader actively shapes and enlarges his or her audience through energy, self-confidence, assertiveness, ambition, and opportunities seized."

It seems that those with unusual abilities to influence the people around them are the ones that are typically seen (and described) as being charismatic. Influence has many dimensions. It can be accomplished by words or deeds. Each of these has a long list of subcategories. It can be the words we use and the passion by which we communicate them, the brilliance of our ideas and visions, and even the form, platform, and media we choose to communicate. It can even be the clothes we wear when communicating. It is who we communicate to and our ability to reach those who can make a difference. All these things, I believe, can be taught. However, to rely solely on teaching carries with it some inherent risks aside from the fact that it is difficult to teach charisma. Am I just splitting hairs? To *acquire* means "to gain possession of, to get by one's own efforts, comes to posses, a thing that one learns over time, to learn or develop a skill or quality." An example would be an "acquired taste referring to something that one learns to like over time."

Since one objective of this book is to look at the challenges faced in imparting (or embedding) these attributes in those we select to be our leaders, we need to distinguish between teaching and learning. It has been said many times that the only person that can change your mind is you. Learning is about changing our minds and behaviors, so it is very much a "me" thing, whereas teaching is a "them" thing. This is not to say that teaching cannot change behaviors or minds, but while there is a correlation, it is not always causal. So we must consider the fact that not everything we teach gets learned, and even less of it gets acquired. If we look at the definition of teaching, we find words like *coach, inform, enlighten, discipline, drill, school,* and *indoctrinate*; it means to share the meaning of imparting information, understanding, or skill. In its broadest and most general use, it can refer to almost any practice that causes others to develop skill or knowledge: to teach children to write, to teach marksmanship to soldiers, or to teach tricks to a dog. Training lays stress on the acquisition of desired skills and oftentimes behaviors through practice, discipline, or the use of rewards or punishments: to train a child to be polite, to train recruits in military skills, or to train a dog to heel. There is a tendency to think of and treat education and training as essentially the same, but there are profound differences. I am reminded of the story of the third-grade child who brought home a note from the teacher tat said, "In accordance with the school district's policy, tomorrow each third grader will receive one hour of sex." Now what is the next word you want to see in that sentence, education or training?

Our approach to solving many organizational problems is by learning through either education and/or training; both of which have a long history with respect to creating and managing change. The first experiments concerning associative learning were conducted by the Russian Ivan Pavlov (conditioned reflex) along with his assistant, Ivan Filippovitch Tolochinov (who referred to it as reflex at a distance), in 1901, and Edward L. Thorndike in the United States. But it was in the writings of John B. Watson that the idea of conditioning became the key learning concept in the developing specialty of comparative psychology and the general approach to psychology that underlay it, behaviorism. The British philosopher Bertrand Russell was an enthusiastic advocate of the importance of Pavlov's work for philosophy of mind. However, critics of the early stimulus-response (S-R) theories, such as Edward C. Tolman, claimed they were overly reductive and ignored a subject's inner activities. Gestalt psychology researchers drew attention to the importance of pattern and form in perception and learning, while structural linguists argued that language learning was grounded in a genetically inherited grammar. Developmental psychologists such as Jean Piaget highlighted stages of growth in learning. More recently, cognitive scientists have explored learning as a form of information processing, while some brain researchers, such as Gerald Maurice Edelman, have proposed that thinking and learning involve an ongoing process of cerebral pathway building.

What we take from all this is that there is some disagreement among scientists going back over one hundred years, and there is work going on at this very moment looking at the brain as distinct from the mind. So all we can do for the time being (as mere humans) is to consider the attributes of the characteristic we want the subject to acquire and whether these attributes (building blocks) can somehow be imparted. So if we can agree that important aspects of charisma are the ability to mobilize people, authenticity, and humility, then reaching a state of "I mean you no harm" seems crucial to becoming a charismatic (non-zero-sum) leader. This is no simple matter, and there are some significant obstacles to overcome. The winning and losing notion is deep-seated in both our psyche and our culture, and changing our attitudes and behaviors takes vision, courage, and persistence. If we are ever to fundamentally alter this disconnect between people and organizations and achieve meaningful and sustainable change in organizational performance without constant turmoil and the all-too-frequent displacement of jobs, we may need to look at the way we approach building organizations and, more importantly, the way we manage them. The challenge is, however, enormous.

Still, in the final analysis, there is a downside to the fixation and credit we give to charismatic leaders. Indeed, some organizations become almost wholly dependent on a single charismatic leader, and when he or she leaves, the organization can go through a serious cultural and financial withdrawal. When Jobs retired the first time at Apple, when Walsh left GE, and when Iacocca left Chrysler, these organizations went through some very difficult times. It begs the question, do charismatic leaders have a genetic flaw? Could it be that the loyalty and passion they inspire is not transferable and they fail to recognize that the organizations they build cannot sustain themselves with the same vigor absent their personal leadership? The point being that followership is not a perk that comes with the position; it must be earned.

Since one measure of charisma is the ability to influence, there is a tendency to think that one's skill at negotiating is a key element of charisma. Since that is a skill that can be taught (with varying degrees of success), then I suppose an argument can be made that at least one characteristic of charisma is teachable. However, even mastery of that skill does little to enhance one's charisma and can even be seen by some as a detriment, since negotiation is oftentimes seen as manipulation. To project charisma (i.e., to be perceived to be charismatic), one must be *believed* to be authentic, trustworthy and truthful, strong, reliable, and possessed of vision and character. Still, taken together, these qualities result in respect but not necessarily charisma. In my opinion, these are difficult (if not impossible) qualities to teach, and so there is reason to think that charisma is a quality one is born with, and the best those who were not born with it can hope for is to build on one's innate self-confidence, communicative skills, creditably, and trust.

Then there is the question, does charisma beget power, or does power beget charisma? On point, while immensely powerful and (by the standards of the day) very successful, I think individuals like Vanderbilt, Rockefeller, and Morgan prove that, in some instances at least, power does not always beget charisma. There are two points about men such as them. First is that they are among the best examples of zero-sum leaders I can think of. Their quest was not so much about money as it was about winning, and second, though we may not identify with their methods, there can be no question of the impact they had on America and in laying its foundation to become the industrial giant of the world. But that is a discussion for another day. However, I am confident that the word *charisma* was never found in a sentence containing any of their names. The good news is that charisma helps but is not an absolute requirement for becoming a non-zero-sum leader.

Chapter Eleven

Stand Up or Sit Down

A great deal of talent is lost in the world for want of courage."

—Sydney Smith

Some of the indispensable characteristics of successful leaders are courage, self-confidence, audacity, decision-making skills, a willingness to take risks, and a readiness to put oneself squarely in the crosshairs. Without these qualities, the rest will basically cancel out. There is much written about risk taking, and it is always part of the corporate curriculum, but I am not entirely convinced that risk *taking* can be taught, especially in a vacuum. In other words, if the culture does not foster these qualities, they will not flourish. It is for this reason that those who have these rare and desirable qualities are most often those who populate the growing ranks of entrepreneurs, not necessarily because they want to get rich, but to release their inner creativity and drive. For some, willingness to accept risk is a gift of birth, for others it is nurtured at an early age by the extended family, and for many it is the result of taking on increased responsibility over time. Others are thrust into positions that leave them no choice.

My first test of will is always to ask those who make the rules for success or failure just how they feel about what they are about to undertake. The prelude to a consulting assignment that had to do with strategic planning for a major corporation was to first ask all the senior executives just how they felt about strategic planning. Tabulating their feelings into a report (which, of course, eliminated any names or titles), I shared this information with the group (including the chairman and the president of the organization) at a retreat that had been planned to discuss the state of strategic planning in the organization. Both the chairman and the president, upon hearing the collective feelings toward the matter, said, "I had no idea that you all felt this way." If you plan to embark on a new path, you had first better be sure that you have an understanding of the collective atti-

tude toward the undertaking for if not supported, it will most surely fail if it is absent both understanding and commitment. This has everything to do with risk taking in an organization. If the culture rewards people for making no errors, you are wasting your time trying to teach people to take risks in the abstract.

Sometimes the situation is such that you have the opportunity to help someone take on risk in a no-risk environment. Such was the case some years back. I was consulting with a company that operates storage or terminal facilities. On the first visit to one of their terminals, I found that the site manager was on his first day of his new job. He had just been appointed to this position, as the previous manager had been summarily dismissed the day before. The new manager (we will call him Bill) had been the supervisor for some time at this terminal, but beyond knowing which value went to which storage tank, he was totally unprepared for his new expanded responsibilities. On his desk was a set of blueprints for a very large and complex modification to the terminal. Bill was not an engineer, and he was absolutely terrified. When I walked in, Bill literally had the phone in hand to call the head office (in another state) to deliver his resignation. As it happened, this company's policy was to have all such site work done by local companies, and while the headquarters employed many engineers, there were none in the field. Bill felt he was in way over his head. I asked him to call the local company that prepared the plans and tell them, up-front, that he was not an engineer and had no idea whether those plans were good or bad. However, the headquarters had trained engineers, and they would know if the plans were good or bad. If it turned out that those were good plans, he would do everything he could to ensure their company got first shot at future work at this terminal, but if it turned out that they were not good plans, he would do whatever he could to make sure that they were not considered for future work here. I had also suggested that he then ask them the following question, "Should I send these plans to the home office?" I was still in his office when Bill made the call, and that was exactly what he told them. There was a pause on the other end of the line. Then the local construction company asked Bill if they could come by and pick up the plans. Bill was a big winner in this situation and discovered a very critical fact. You don't have to be the expert to be in control, and creating situations where there are no losers is empowering even when you make yourself vulnerable. Indeed, that will often be the case. Bill put a big target on his back, and it could have turned out otherwise, but most of the time you will be surprised at what being up-front and vulnerable can accomplish. As Mark Twain said, "Courage is resistance to fear, mastery of fear, not absence of fear."

Sometimes there will be an opportunity to encourage people to take a risk by taking the bullet for them, or at least being prepared to. Let's be frank, most organizations are not really good at encouraging risk taking, and employees know that. After all, how many people do you know who got fired for not taking risks? So how can a non-zero-sum leader support risk-taking behaviors? An industrial engineer was working on a new layout for the labeling operation in a large food-processing company where I was the CFO. As I had been a senior industrial engineer in an earlier life, I had some ideas of my own. I could have just critiqued his plan, but I wasn't looking to make it mine, and I certainly didn't want to take ownership. I wanted him to stand up for what I was sure he knew what the best solution looked like, and it was not the plan on his worktable. You see, he had not been asked for the best solution but rather to rearrange the operation to make it more efficient. I asked him if this was the plan he would propose to management if the only constraints he had were the walls, the roof, and floor. The reply came swiftly: "No," he said. I asked him to draw up that plan. He did, and the cost to fund his new plan was $2 million, but the payback was eighteen months as the new equipment he proposed took less manpower to produce more throughputs. The only question that came up at the Board meeting was "Why didn't we do this sooner?" Yes, I had to give him permission and cover to take a risk, but it gave him the chance to put his talent and expertise on the line, and I think that with the next opportunity to come along, he might just stick his head out a little further than he would have because of the positive experience of risking and winning.

It is possible, even in a risk-averse organization, to allow (or even encourage) people to stand up. Sometimes, however, it takes more than helping them to understand or to get in touch with their risk-taking profile by falling backward into someone's waiting arms. Sometimes you have to give them both the tools needed and an appropriate opportunity to take on risk. Here is another example from the food industry: Asked to help improve performance and reduce costs of production, I decided upon a strategy of letting the department supervisors do it. After all, they knew a lot more about their own operations than I did or ever could. However, there were some things they needed to know in order to accomplish what management had asked for. Things like ratio-delay analysis, net present value, trend line analysis, and how to sell your ideas, all skills they would need to successfully accomplish the goals they would set for themselves. We met one night a week, usually over dinner, with the supervisors involved *and* the appropriate vice president from each company. You see, it was critical to the supervisors' success that the vice presidents had the same knowledge going in as the supervisors because I didn't want the supervisors, when it came time to make the changes, to run up against an "I don't understand what you are talking about" situation. The supervisors did all the work, but the vice presidents shared in the understanding. The first assignment was to look for a change project in their department (or someone else's with that department's permission) that could make a contribution to savings. The problem setup was a risk-reward plan. Each participant was to get cash reward as a result of the savings they produced divided by the payroll in that department. In this way, a small improvement in a small department had more value than a small improvement in a large department. To get started, they first had to identify a meaningful change opportunity. Here is why they needed to learn the principles of ratio-delay analyses. These instructional sessions were attended by the vice presidens. I had located some old 8mm movies that walked them through the process of making these studies. They then took those tools and went out into their workplaces to discover where the best opportunities to exploit were. That process took a few weeks, and then, having isolated some of the opportunities, we spent time working through the problem of costing any investment required and the resulting savings using present-value calculations. At each step in the process up through and including how to make the sale to the department vice president, they were given the support they needed. It was a very successful undertaking. At the conclusion of the program, we had a presentation dinner with, of course, the vice presidents present. Now came the part I did not anticipate. The cash award (which roughly equaled a month's pay for the best outcome) was handed to the first-place winner (all got an award). When that individual turned to his vice president and said, "I don't want this, please take it and use it to put more people through this program." I almost cried. However, recovering quickly, I suggested we hold that over until after dinner as I suspected that some of the others might not want to give back their awards. But this reaffirmed my belief that people really want to make a difference and, given the chance and the tools to do it, will respond in ways that you will find truly astonishing.

In a leadership context, courage is most often (or should be) evidenced by those you influence. From the person with a stack of blueprints on his desk to the shift manager in data entry, there are endless opportunities to help others and the organization to grow. We need to remember that courage is only one side of the coin; the other side of the coin is risk. What fuses these two sides together is *confidence*. Absent confidence, courage will never exhibit itself. In the case above with the plant supervisors, note that I did not (could not) give them courage. That would be like my changing your mind, which, of course, only you can do. What one can do is to provide the tools (or situations) that offer the opportunity for others to gain confidence in their own abilities. The notion that one can teach confidence seems a bit far-fetched; people need to experience it. As said earlier, change lies in the difference between teaching and learning. Teaching is something I do to you, whereas learning is something you do to you.

The triad of courage/risk/confidence can manifest itself in small ways or in big ways. My personal test was to tell myself that when I no longer felt I could disagree (in an appropriate way and place) with the president and CEO, my value to the firm was diminished. Imagine if your team had that attitude and freedom. What great and exciting break-throughs you could accomplish. Next time you have the answer, think about how you can hand off the ball to someone else who might need (and welcome) the chance to step up. The answer may not be yours, but if it solves the problem, does it really matter that it is not yours? When I took my first job as an industrial engineer, I read all the books on the subject to find out what I was supposed to do.  They all had one central theme, which was to find "the one best way" and then teach everyone how to do it that way. However, it wasn't long before I learned that there is no such thing as one best way. What is best for one may not be the best for another, and so one needed to look and take into consideration other best ways. So it is the non-zero-sum leader who opens the door to the discovery of others' courage and to seek out and create those opportunities for them to step up.

CHAPTER TWELVE

Why Leads to Understanding
Why Not Leads to Solutions

> My experience has shown me that the people
> who are exceptionally good in business aren't so
> because of what they know but because of their
> insatiable need to know more.
>
> —Michael Gerber

The non-zero-sum leader is always on the edge and never satisfied with what is but looks for what could be. Absent a challenge, non-zero-sum leaders would dry up and blow away. They are always challenging and looking for the "How can this be better?" They are proactive and don't wait around for the problem to become evident, and they ask the kind of "why not" questions that expose opportunities.

While I was working at a food processing company (in 1973, a time when canned fruit was the only option to fresh fruit once fresh fruits were out of season), I asked the executive vice president why he thought people who liked fresh fruit didn't buy canned fruit when fresh was not available. His reply was "You don't understand. People who eat fresh fruit don't eat canned fruit." My follow-up question was "Did you ever wonder why not?" As a buyer of canned fruit myself,

I thought it had everything to do with what the industry does to the canned fruit. The prevailing practice was to take the very best quality fruit and add a *lot* of sugar based on the theory that since they can sell it for more, they can afford to add more sugar. Indeed, in those days (and maybe still today), the choice fruit was packed in extra heavy syrup (code words for lots of sugar)—ugh. Our personal practice was to buy the extra-heavy sugar item as it was the best quality fruit and then take it home and rinse off all (or as much as we could) the sugar. I suggested that fresh fruit buyers might like quality fruit packed in water or even in its own juice. Next year, the company came out with those two options (the very first company to do so), and for the next two decades, this was the fastest-growing segment of the canned-fruit market. This is every CFO's dream: a product welcomed by consumers, lower cost of production, and a higher shelf price.

I recall when I was consulting in an order processing department that one of the things I wanted to know was how many credit invoices were being issued, as that was an important data point in how well the invoicing system was working. We (the department supervisor and I) walked over to the desk of the person responsible for processing these credits and asked to see the credit orders she had to process. She pointed to her in-basket, which had some ten or fewer invoices, and I thought that was extremely low, far below what I would have expected in such a large organization. More often than not, one would look no further when things seem to be going well. Why would you want any additional information when it can't get any better? But I asked, "Are these *all* the credits you have to process?" She replied no and opened her lower desk drawer, which was filled to capacity with credits that she had to research. If you really want to know how things are going, you need to look over, under, and beyond, as determination trumps feeling good every time.

Wanting to see how effectively the warehouse inventory control system was working, I randomly pulled several punched cards from the warehouse location card file and asked if someone would take me to the locations indicated on the cards. One out of every three locations was correct; we could not find the other two. To this day, it amazes me how superficially we manage our responsibilities. We want things to go well, and the less we dig, the better things appear. One of the fundamental rules of leadership, per the late Dr. George Odorine, was "Never let your boss be surprised." How many surprises are lurking just below the surface on your desk or in your department? You have so many opportunities for improvement that they likely could fill your calendar for the rest of the year, and what better way to fill it, for as Leonardo da Vinci said, "It had long since come to my attention that people of accomplishment rarely sat back and let things happen to them. They went out and happened to things." You will be surprised by what you can accomplish and contribute once you set about it. Examine what you do and why and ask, what if? Set a goal, make a plan, and *become the you* that excites those around you. Own your success.

My first job out of college was as a math and science teacher at a junior high school in California. In that state, the learning objective for the entire year was to teach the students fractions. I simply could not figure out how to take an entire year teaching fractions. I decided to take a different approach. I still had to complete the seventh-grade learning objective, but there was nothing I knew of that said that was *all* I *could* do. It was in this, my first job, that I learned that we consistently (and with grave consequences) underestimate people's abilities and, worse yet, their genuine desire to be their best. Within the first few months, I started giving short verbal quizzes at the start of each class. I might ask the students to add 1/7 + 3/49 + 2/21. The only rule in these quizzes is that the student could not use paper or pencil. Within about five seconds, virtually all the students would raise their hands, indicating they had the answer. Incidentally, raising them like shot out of a gun with great confidence and enthusiasm, not simply "I know the answer." This was proof enough for me to plunge ahead. By the time of the midterm exams, one of the questions on the test was a square that was seven inches on a side and had a circle inside that touched the inside edge of the square and the question was, what is the area of the circle? The answer did not require the use of fractions. We went on from there to questions like the cylinder on the well crank handle had a radius of 6 inches and it took fourteen turns of the handle to get my water to the top of the well. How far down is it to the water? The point of this example is that people can and want to be challenged, and as a leader, that is a (perhaps the) key component of your job. Think about how you felt when you were challenged with a seemingly awesome task and you pulled it off. I'll bet it was infinitely more satisfying than after you had cleared your in-basket of credit invoices. It was Jim Rohn who said, "You want to set a goal that is big enough that in the process of achieving it you become someone worth becoming."

Yet another example of how knowing what holds you back from setting and achieving your stretch objectives, the kind of objectives that can really make a difference and can lead you to discover what true leadership is all about. Consulting with a large food-processing company, I asked all the vice presidents (managing multiple plants in multiple states) to write down the six or so things that prevented them from having their perfect day. The reasons varied, but one item was on all their lists—the weather. So we spent some time taking that idea apart, piece by piece. There were, at that time, numerous (and very successful) experiments growing product in (nonhydroponic) enclosed environments. The results were impressive, yielding the equivalent of twenty-six acres grown out of doors for every one acre grown in these enclosed environments. You could also harvest products, such as tomatoes, two to three times a week, year around. Of course, the plants were watered using the more efficient drip system instead of inefficient overhead or irrigation systems. Because they were indoors, they needed very little (or no) herbicides or pesticides. A major cost factor in processing tomatoes is getting the water out of the tomatoes to create tomato paste.

This cost is inversely related to the percentage of solids in the tomatoes. Tomatoes grown in the open field might, on average, be expected to yield 5.5 percent to upward of almost 8 percent solids. If grown in a contained and controlled environment, it should be possible to average a yield of 10 percent or better, significantly reducing the cost of production. There are other major cost factors, such as the need to store essentially a year's worth of product because the crops' growing season is much shorter than the purchasing season. There are three costs associated with this: financing the stored product, building facilities big enough to house this entire seasonal output, and the cost of ending up having a product no one wants while not having a product they do want. If you think it is difficult trying to forecast the weather a year in advance, forecasting the market a year ahead with anything even close to 100 percent accuracy is no cakewalk. So you lose money on both ends, not having the product the market wants and being stuck with the product the market does not want. Now imagine a thousand hothouses surrounding a single plant that is continuously fed product and runs all year long. Imagine the value (cost savings) of keeping the same (experienced) staff year-round instead of rehiring each packing year, as the seasons are only three to four months long. The plant doesn't have to shut down for eight or nine months. This factor alone has major advantages and cost savings. So you ask, why don't they do it this way? As you have no doubt guessed by now, it has absolutely nothing to do with the weather! The reason it is not done this way is that much of the tomato production in the United States is done by cooperatives. Cooperatives are owned by the farmers who deliver their product to the plant for processing and share in the proceeds from the sale of the finished products. However, the farmers in any one year may not (as in highly unlikely) be the exact same farmers that delivered their product to that plant last year. So each year, the new owners form a new pool, and the federal government says that you can't pass on any losses from one pool to another. The rub is you now have four plants (because you need that many to process all the tomatoes you get over a three- or four-month period), and if you want to close the three plants you don't need, under this system, who will bear the costs of closing those three plants? So what was the purpose of this exercise? To make the point that, often, what we think is an issue turns out not to be the problem, but you may uncover a better way to accomplish your goal if you start by looking at what it is that prevents your desired state. In this case, it would take action by the federal Ggovernment, so why not spend your time there instead of cursing the weather? First, you need to clear away the fog and confusion surrounding the problem, and then you need the determination to see your solution through. As Ogwo David Emenike said, "There is a thin line between the impossible and the possible—that is determination."

When you next go to work (or better still while at home), take the time to write down the main issues (obstacles) that prevent you, your team, or your department from having a perfect day. Picture yourself going to work and, after your walk-around, concluding that you could go back home. What five or six things would you look at to make that determination? Next, write down how you know that these, rather than some other related factor, actually impact your operations. Do you have some measurements that tell you all of what you need to know about the extent these factors affect your operation? Do you have some (even if crude) measure of relative impact? Or do you just *think* they have an impact? Do you control any of these factors? Can you influence and either eliminate or redirect these impediments? What do you have to trade for changes that others (people or departments) may need to make? Which would have the greatest benefit or which would be the easiest? Don't go after it all at one time because sometimes fixing one thing may change your ordering of the remaining priorities on your list. Karen Lamb has some advice for you on such matters: "A year from now you may wish you had started today."

The paradigm shift starts by rethinking your notions about control. A good place to begin is by focusing on the outcomes rather than processes. We need to become better at setting out the objectives and taking the time to communicate our expectations and less time on putting the train back on the track. But let's be honest, most of us would rather people figure it out on their own. We don't like to criticize, are not very good at it, and even uncomfortable doing it.

We think professionals should know how without being told. Many of us were raised in an environment where the norm was telling people what is wrong rather than telling them what right would look like. Sound familiar? Sound a little like the T-shirt that said, "My Name Is Not No No."

CHAPTER THIRTEEN

The Best Way Forward Is Not Always a Straight Line

Determine that the thing can and shall be done
and then find the way.

—Abraham Lincoln

Is there any difference between zero-sum creativity and non-zero-sum creativity? Certainly the zero-sum people discussed in the chapter on charisma displayed behaviors characteristic of creative people. A closer look, however, suggests that while they were certainly innovative, they were not necessarily creative. Creativity means to bring into existence, whereas innovation means to make changes of methods. Since, for the most part, they took existing things (shipping, railroading, oil products, steel making, etc.) and found new ways to combine or take over existing companies so as to maximize power and profits, it seems to me that creativity is not an entirely appropriate label in their cases.

My experience is that there are some not insignificant differences between the zero-sum and the non-zero-sum leaders in terms of their approach to creativity. Of note is the fact that the innovation of those referred to earlier left a good many (dead) bodies lying around. Moreover, their focus was all about "What can I do to increase my winnings" (not simply in terms of money, although there was a lot of that made) but in terms of power. The Great Depression of 1873–1879 was in large part caused by the collapse of railroad stocks. The industry had vastly overbuilt and that, combined with reduced reliance on rail (and more on pipelines) to move kerosene for lamps, led to the 1873 sell-off of railroad stocks, which put thousands of small companies out of business and led to a deep and long depression. Then, in 1878, along came Edison with a filament that would last for one hundred hours, and the electric light slowly began to replace the kerosene lamp. This left Rockefeller with a big problem. But as fate (or as some would have it, luck) had it, people in Europe were perfecting a device called the internal combustion engine. It was in 1861 when Nikolaus August Otto patterned the first commercially viable internal combustion engine. The first workable internal engine was actually invented in 1850 by the French Engineer J. J. Étienne Lenoir, but it lacked Otto's carburetor to make it practical. It was in 1867 at the World's Fair in Paris that Otto's two-stroke engine won the gold medal. During the lamp years, a by-product of making kerosene was a substance called gasoline. It was a useless product and was simply dumped in the rivers of Cleveland. It was toward the end of this Depression that Rockefeller and his kerosene business were facing the prospect of increasing competition from the electric light. But as it turned out, this waste product (gasoline) was the perfect fuel to power the new internal combustion engines.

Zero-sum leaders tend to be linear in their approach and reductive (rather than systemic) in thinking. This manifests itself in problem solving instead of problem elimination. This may sound like splitting hairs, but let's take a look at the difference it can make in how problems are framed.

As Bernice Fitz-Gibbon said, "Creativity often consists of merely turning up what is already there." She went on to point out "that right and left shoes were a new idea only a little more than a century ago."

Back to the business of this chapter. As I said earlier, framing is the key to the practice of viewing from the top of the box. Seeing from outside the box still leaves one with at least one blind spot—the box you just stepped out of; whereas on top of the box, nothing

obstructs the view, and one can see all the way to the horizon line. Let's look at a challenge faced some years ago. Production and payroll information was entered by a keypunch operator, which was time consuming, costly, and the information had to be first keypunched using a machine like this into a card (as seen below), and then another operator had to verify the original keypunch operator's work, which doubled the time (and cost) it took to enter data. For those of you who are not familiar with punched cards, they were of two types. The

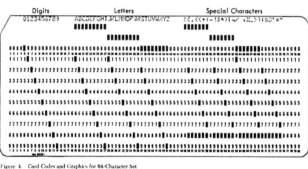

Figure 4. Card Codes and Graphics for 64-Character Set

most common had eighty columns with small rectangular punched holes in columns of twelve punches with each column identifying a single bit (or character) in the computer. The other type was a ninety-column card (again with twelve punches each) but with round holes. Each had advantages but both took time and labor to enter the information. This process meant a plant manager (in this case with as many as five thousand seasonal employees) had to wait until after the next day's shift to find out what happened two days ago. As you can imagine, it was difficult for the plant manager to make the necessary changes to correct any problems since the information was submitted after the shift and processed the next day; thus, the manager got the results two shifts later. In addition, the information he finally got

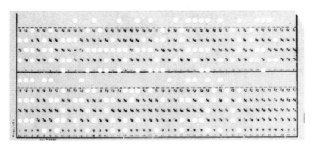

didn't really tell him what he did wrong (or right) two days ago. As we discussed in chapter 8, the other part of the puzzle was the convoluted system of reporting cost of production, which had very little to do with production costs and nothing to do with how (or what) the manager actually managed.

There was more than one issue here, but let's go first to the issue that needed a solution. How do you get information to the plant manager on a timely basis, say before his next shift starts? Simple, you say, just triple the number of keypunch (*and* key verify) operators and build another office to house them all. What else can you do? After all, the machines need these cards to produce the report. I submit that is focusing on the problem, but what I wanted to do was look at the system. I wasn't interested in how to fix the problem; I wanted to look at how to eliminate the problem. It was true that the machines needed cards, and they needed holes in the cards in order to be able to read them. What if there were a third kind of card, one with really big holes and not necessarily in neat columns? Indeed, when I took my strange cards (which looked very different from the cards shown above) to several companies to have them put through their machines, they all said the same thing, "Our machines can't read those cards." I asked, "How do your machines read cards?" They all replied, "By reading light passing through holes." Meaning *their* holes. And I said, "My cards have holes, so please put them through your machine." Of course their machines read the cards just fine. Now it was true (and I knew this would be the case) that their machines had no idea *what* they were reading, but that didn't matter because I already had a program written that would tell their machines what they were reading. What was it about my cards that was so different? The card stock had been preprinted with a matrix of products and jobs (processes). They had been prepunched (by machines but not by keypunch operators and not keyverifier operators) with the employee number and shift and picked up by the employees at the beginning of their shifts. In the matrix were boxes indicating various products and jobs, but nothing was punched in that area. Instead, each foreman was given a special conductor punch made specifically to span multiple rows and columns so that the shift foreman could then, during his or her shift, go around the department and punch (using this special punch they all had) the product and job that person was working on. These holes made by the foreman were much bigger than the keypunched holes, but that was by design; it was important that the foreman not have to be very accurate in punching the holes. In fact, the holes could be partway into the next box, and the algorithm that had been programmed was such that it could read the cards with less than 0.10 percent (1/10 of 1 percent) error rate (in such cases, the machine was programmed to reject that card, and only in those few cases would the card be given to an operator to manually correct). This approach allowed us to leapfrog the keypunch and key verify operations altogether and get the information at the beginning of the next shift, enabling the company to greatly reduce the cost of production. I think Jim Henson got it just right when he said, "If you learn too much of what others have done—you may tend to take the same direction as everybody else."

Yet another classic example of linear thinking was the problem facing the vice president of distribution. This company produced the vast majority of its products for other companies, so the inventory included not just their products but unlabeled canned products that would later have the labels applied and put in boxes for the companies they would ultimately be sold to. If any one of these items (labels or boxes) were out of stock, the order could not be shipped. The term used to describe this situation was *dirty orders*. This situation did cause problems, but standing on top of my box, I could see over the problem to the objective, which was really to fill every order as received and shipped in accordance with the customer's request. My task was to create a system that made sure that all (or at least the vast majority of) orders we received were clean. Taking on the assignment, I asked for one caveat, and that was to also create a computer model that could be used to simulate the distribution center in order to test the effect of solving the problem. It was a simple step to solve the inventory problem; I just had IT take all of last year's orders and remove all the error codes. Now we had a full year's worth of orders without so much as a single problem. We then ran those orders through the computer model and found that the worst nightmare was to solve that label and box problem because it would flood the available equipment. The result would have been disastrous in terms of on-time deliveries. We then undertook an evaluation of the equipment needed to meet the objective, not just to "solve the problem." As Jiddu Krishnamurti said, "Freedom from the desire for an answer is essential to the understanding of a problem."

It is my contention that the greatest single obstacle to creativity is rules. Rules are the shackles of the mind; they are what rein in creativity. As Jim Gilmore said, "If the rules of creativity are the norm for a company, creative people will be the norm." How does this play out in meeting everyday challenges? Some years back I was in New York and wanted to visit the Met to view their early American art collection. Arriving at the opening hour, I was informed that because of budget cuts, the American wing was closed that morning. Disappointed but not dismayed, I took off for a meeting in Connecticut and returned the next afternoon only to be told that due to budget cuts, the American wing was closed that afternoon.

Some clever person had the idea that rotating the closings made more sense than a consistent policy regarding closings. I would not be dissuaded. I asked the information attendant to connect me by phone to the person in charge of the American collection. She did that for me, and I explained my interest and passion and that the New York Met arguably had the very best collection, and since I was from Nevada, my chances of seeing it again were limited. My proposal was that if I could be permitted to see it, I would pledge my firstborn to the museum. Having never had *that* offer before, she asked me to wait a minute and soon came back with a solution. She had found a docent that agreed to take me to see the collection.

It is oftentimes better to go around the problem than to try to plow through; when the road ahead is blocked, try the side streets.

The thing about rules (in business) is that they are not a function of nature but are made up to fit a certain occasion. I once found myself in disagreement with a very large corporation's policy that was neither useful nor responsible and was damaging to our firm and others. I called the company and asked why they were pursuing this course, and the individual replied, "It is our company policy," to which I replied, "Companies don't make policy, people do." I then asked who he thought decided on the policy, and he said, "I guess the president." I then asked to speak to the president, and he gave me the president's number. No sooner had I hung up then I called the president and explained my position regarding the policy. He asked that I send him my objections and suggestions in writing, which I did. Three months or so later, the company changed its policy. A non-zero-sum leader does not get stymied by rules; indeed, such a leader looks past rules to what the objective is and sets sight on that rather than the obstacle. There is nothing magical or impermeable about rules; they are made up and can therefore be unmade if they get in the way of creativity or progress.

CHAPTER FOURTEEN

The Global Road Ahead

> Don't underestimate the power of your vision to change the world. Whether that world is your office, your community, an industry or a global movement, you need to have a core belief that what you contribute can fundamentally change the paradigm or way of thinking about problems.
>
> —Leroy Hood

But Does All This Really Matter to America and Its Middle Class?

Let's continue with our example and see whether these structural changes actually create any losers (in terms of U.S. jobs), and if so, how many? Did you know, Bob, that in 1979, GM's hourly workforce (i.e., middle class) was 468,000, and it is now (thirty-five years later) 52,000? No doubt productivity improvement (e.g., robotics) have contributed to that drop, but they do have another 55,000 employees now in China. Add to that, GM also employs about 15,000 people in its Mexico operations. Another 105,000 people work at plants that supply GM, which spends about $14 billion a year on purchasing in the country.

No matter how you slice it, Bob, that's a lot of bodies. You know, it reminds me of the ancient practice of bloodletting as a cure for sickness. That didn't work then and it won't work now. Neither GM nor Ford can cure their collective ills by operating over a dozen plants in China, sucking the blood out of America. I grant you they have made a good deal of profit from these operations, but the time will come, I believe, in the not-very-distant future, when China will make good on its determination to go global. And once they are producing products that are as good as those produced in the rest of the world, they will start exporting them. GM and Ford are making that not just possible but probable. I do not buy into the argument of Willem and Michael Sorell (as written in the *Harvard Business Review*) that "given their current position, Chinese brands are unlikely to be dominant anytime soon—even if China's economy becomes the world's biggest." This view assumes facts not in evidence. I am in the James Tusk George camp: "More likely, at some point China will think that its reputation of manufacturing is good enough so that it can launch its own brands." I think that John Scully got it right when he said, "The future belongs to those who see possibilities before they become obvious."

While Backstage

So where does this take us? Is this all Detroit's fault or Apple's or GE's? We need to dig deeper, Bob, to understand what it is that drives Detroit. I think we need to look to Wall Street. It is not that I think Wall Street is somehow inherently evil or bad. No, I just think they have gotten very, very good at what they do and what investors expect them to do. Yes, government policies have a lot to do with it (highest corporate tax rate in the world, too many regulations and too many regulators, etc.) but while that has contributed to creating a challenging business environment, and perhaps encouraged outsourcing, it is not the root source of what is going on in our major goods-producing companies. We need to look at the cause and effect that Wall Street has on our economy. We, you and I, Bob, invest our savings in various instruments that we hope will pay us a reasonable return. We haven't been able to do that in fixed instruments (bonds, treasuries, etc.) lately, and banks are paying less than the rate of inflation, so we have few options other than Wall Street products. The results (not necessarily the returns) are predictable in that the trading houses and funds are all trying to capture customers (and profits), and the way they do that is by outperforming their competition. That is precisely what we want them to do, and the result is that Wall Street is ruthless when it comes to tolerating poor performance. This is what pushes Detroit to invest its resources in places like China instead of the United States. Without much in the way of patient money, corporations have no wiggle room, and they must beat their numbers quarter after quarter after quarter. To be fair (and balanced), Wall Street did not invent this model; it goes all the way back to pre-biblical times. However, it was the creativity of the Italians in the sixteenth century that launched many of today's sophisticated trading instruments. Then Amsterdam, at the beginning of the seventeenth century, became the center of investment. It was here that trade in derivatives, options, and repos were firmly established. Amsterdam did however (in 1620) decide to ban one new invention that remains as controversial today as it was back then—short selling.

If We Can't (Don't Want to) Change Wall Street, Where Does That Leave Us?

We are where we are, and the question is, do we need to right our course, or is the fast-food industry growing fast enough to employ all the displaced middle-class Americans? William Jennings Bryan gave us one option: "Destiny is not a matter of chance, but of choice. Not something to wish for, but to attain." So how do we correct this? Given our current strategies (?) of government, those of corporate America, and those of Wall Street, is it even possible to avoid becoming the world's second-largest (and second-class) economy? There are already a number of fundamental changes going on in the financial markets that suggest it may be too late. Despite claims that the American dollar is still the world's currency of choice, the fact is that Russia and China are no longer exchanging goods in dollars. The Middle East is using a basket of currencies, and China is doing business with its Asian neighbors in local currencies and not dollars. Some countries no longer take dollars from American tourists, and many of those that do limit the number of dollars they will (in many cases are legally allowed to) accept. As the United States continues to print dollars, it will continue to devalue its global worth, and as the debt climbs relentlessly upward, there seems no end to the manufacturing of more and more dollars of less and less value.

Corporations (at least the larger ones) have an answer, and they are pursuing it with a vengeance—China and, gaining rapidly, Mexico. American corporations are taking every advantage of labor at rates as low as $0.51 an hour. Of course, those American companies that create the most jobs, the small- to middle-sized companies, don't typically have the luxury of outsourcing to these countries. Therein lies the real ticking time bomb. I firmly believe that Detroit (and most of the one-time industrial giants) cannot effectively reconstitute their U.S. operations by simply adding water to shuttered plants to regenerate a likeness of their former selves. Once they start shuttering American plants in favor of the low cost of labor elsewhere, there is little chance they will (or even can) ever pull back, especially once Detroit starts importing cars made in China. Once China has exploited their auto advantage, they will turn to smaller ventures. U.S. companies in the $25,000,000 to $100,000,000 range may be seen as small- to midsize companies in the United States, but in China, they would be seen as prime candidates to exploit. Besides, China needs to distribute its manufacturing to offset the population flow from the land to its major cities and to spread the production and wealth to the provinces. Indeed, as the first step in that direction, China is now considering letting those that farm the land own the land, land which is currently owned by the government and leased to the farmer, land on which the farmer and his family can live but have never been able to sell. Currently, they can sell the housing structure in which they live but not the land on which it sits. Since whoever buys the house currently has to get permission from the government to farm the land, home ownership is not a vehicle for building personal worth. This change would break the chains binding hundreds of thousands of young people to the land and free them to work in the factories, not unlike what happened in America during the late 1800s and early 1900s. China's future (and prosperity) does not lie in the land but in manufacturing. If our politicians think that a reduced corporate tax rate will lure manufacturers back to the United States, they are deluding themselves.

What Are the Options?

When labor costs are 10 percent to 20 percent of those in the United States, it will take a complete rethinking of what it is that makes capitalism thrive if we are to stand toe-to-toe with a determined, single-minded dictatorship that can (and does) control the means of production, the costs, and the pricing thereof. It is time to take a fresh look at what the practices and policies are that have made American manufacturing the most productive in the world. As Mick Ukleja and Robert Lorber have said, "Reflection is looking in so you can look out with a broader, bigger, and more accurate perspective." Just what might we expect if we were to set our minds to "landing a man on the moon and returning him safely to the earth" by the end of the decade? Oops, Bob, that one had already been done. But is it possible (and necessary) for America to set itself a new vision, one that fits its needs for this decade and beyond? I think that it is possible, but it will be even more challenging and harder than putting a man on the moon, as we continue to ratchet up that which makes us ever more noncompetitive. Bob, let's look at some anticompetitive pressure points. Just one seemingly small (but current) example: BART (the San Francisco Bay Area Rapid System) unions are asking for a 20.1 percent increase in pay over the next three years. Now what has that to do with our ability to compete globally? I think it has a whole lot more to do with our ability to compete globally than a high-speed rail line from ninety miles north of Los Angeles to somewhere near San Francisco. We continue to operate as if what we do (often in response to union demands) has no impact on our ability to attract and retain a viable manufacturing base. When wages in the public sector increase, there follows a push in the private sector. Strategically, raising wages in the public sector first makes sense, as they provide public services and therefore the resistance is minimized as these services affect the voter's ability to (in this case) get to work. So ratcheting up public wages builds the pressure on companies to follow suit. Add to that the push for a *minimum* wage of $15 per hour, which would apply even to the seventeen-year-old who dropped out of high school. He or she would make more than a starting teacher in Arizona, Idaho, Maine, Missouri, Mississippi, Montana, North Carolina, North Dakota, Oklahoma, and South Dakota and just very slightly less than a dozen other states. These increases contribute to (cause) the situations we experienced in the seventies when the global competitive spiral first began, and it took the better part of two decades to reset the scales. We have made little progress in leveling the cost scales, but by taking manufacturing out of the one side (the United States) and putting it into the other side (i.e., outsourcing), we have been able to maintain a position of relative competitiveness albeit at a cost of millions of American jobs. For a country that says it wants to entice companies to come (or come back) to the U.S. $15 an hour will not be much (any) inducement. There are countries that offer huge wage differentials. Even the average Chinese factory worker now makes $3.40 per hour, up several fold in the past ten years, Indonesia's average hourly wage is $1.08, Vietnam is 84¢, Mexico is 62¢, while India is 31¢ per hour.

There is some good news on the manufacturing front "as Toyota, Airbus, Siemens, and Rolls-Royce move more production to the U.S. for export," as BCG partner Michael Zinser says. Maybe the European Union is America's salvation? This shift is, of course, due primarily to rising wages in some Western European countries, which makes the United States seem more cost-effective and, in a very few cases, a less restrictive place to do business. Still, when looking at other options, the rate of wage increases in the EU last year was (on average) only 1.9 percent, and I would expect more production to migrate to Eastern Europe to take advantage of the even lower rates and increases there. According to a recent report by Frost & Sullivan, the electronics manufacturing services (EMS) market in Eastern Europe will grow from about $9 billion in 2006 to nearly $24 billion in 2013. This, according to Frost & Sullivan, is not a surprise as Eastern Europe has a culture and infrastructure conducive to volume manufacturing and good availability of skilled labor, flexible employment policies and contracts, good cooperation with customs and other authorities, and a high degree of professionalism. So the ripple effect of a 20-plus percent increase over three years will undoubtedly affect the rest of society. Add to that the ever-increasing burden of swelling retirement benefits for the public sector and the cost burden to those in the private sector. To assume that 20 percent increases will not have any impact on our ability to compete with the rest of the world or that what the rest of the world does is naive. This is a peculiarly American mind-set. The classic example is the question once put to me by a friend in Europe "do you know what people who speak three languages are called?" the answer is tri-lingual, "do you know what people who speak two languages are called?" The answer is bi-lingual. "Do you know what people who speak one language are called? His answer was American. It seems a small thing, but it speaks volumes about our vision of the world and our place in it. To think that constant pressure on wages and costs (no matter if it happens in San Francisco or Detroit) does not affect our overall competitiveness is foolish and shortsighted. Unions need to come to their senses; this is not the forties or fifties. They need to focus on the long-term to best serve their members, and that means helping to retain American jobs. High wages are great, but only if there are jobs. It reminds me of the lady who asked the price of the store's bananas and was told they were $1.50 a pound. She responded that across the street, they were only $1.25 a pound, and so the clerk asked her why she didn't buy them there. She replied that they were out of bananas. The clerk replied, "Our bananas are only $1.00 a pound when we are out of them." It is the age-old formula for profit; it is margin times turn-over. It is one thing to have high margins (in this case, wages) but if there is little turnover (fewer jobs), there will be no profit, and there goes the American middle class.

We Need to Think Big to Make a Difference

On today's news, one of the commentators said that "America always negotiates from a position of strength." Sorry, Bob, but I find that almost laughable. As a one-time navy pilot, I am sure you are aware that we are cutting back the number of aircraft carriers in our fleet. Have you seen this new (the first of five) Chinese aircraft carriers? This path we are on (defense, economy, competition, debt management, jobs, a polarized government, etc.) leads me to conclude that by the end of this decade, absent a commitment to alter course, there will, in fact, be only one superpower, and it won't be America. In colloquial terms, what we have is the makings of a perfect storm, plus an 8.9 earthquake and a tsunami thrown in for good measure. Clearly, Bob, we need to get our house in order and quickly. Imagine when the interest rates return to historical norms. With a projected $20 trillion in debt (excluding the federal unfunded liabilities that exceed $127 trillion), a return to historic interest rates will bring our total *interest payments* on the debt to something between $850 billion to $1 trillion by 2016. Once you have to keep borrowing just to pay the interest, which, of course, is what we are doing, all it is does serve to add further to the debt. We are already on a steep downhill slope with little prospect of turning things around. Frankly, I think we have already passed the tipping point. We need politicians and CEOs who think in systemic terms and factor in all the stakeholders, not just the stockholders. We need to forsake some of these short-term profits to protect (what is left of) our manufacturing base. When you are in a hole over your head, stop digging.

I Choose to Think So

Can it be done? I think it can, but it will take a legion of (non-zero-sum) leaders with the vision, the courage, the drive and determination of Columbus, the wisdom of Socrates, and the patience of Job. It will be painful, very painful. Think Greece. Of course, one option is to simply devalue the dollar by 20 per-

cent to 50 percent. If we are to hold on to our manufacturing base, it seems to me imperative that we need to be in a position, within the next five years, to fend off (or at least hold our own against) the inevitable importation of Chinese-made cars. Can Detroit do that on its own, and does Detroit even see it coming? I doubt it, but even if they do, Detroit cannot continue to pour capital into China at the current rate and also protect their U.S. operations. And in any event, should America risk its manufacturing future on Detroit's bet? After all, Detroit's car of the future is the Volt, which General Motors CEO Dan Akerson described as "not a step forward, but a leap forward." As compared to what? The Morrison electric car that was built in 1891 could carry six to twelve passengers and only needed to be charged every fifty miles, which is less frequently than the Volt. It has been said the Morrison was actually completed in 1887 and was driven in a Des Moines parade in 1888. This means that what Detroit has accomplished in the last 122 years is to make an electric car that goes five times faster (but no further) than the one built in 1887–1891. One thing that comes to (my) mind is using the creativity and resources of the people that have solved the impossible before. In fact, NASA has been doing that for fifty years. Let the National Academy for Scientific Advancement do what they do better than anyone else. Give NASA a new life and a new challenge: design the car of the future—fifty miles per gallon, using whatever mix of power technology meets that criteria, seats five, is not necessarily fast but reasonably comfortable, good looking, and which can be sold profitably in the United States for *under* $10,000. How about a $100 billion stimulus for NASA, for America, and *for the United States*! My overriding concern is what I call the Chinese black hole, like its interstellar cousins, sucking in everything in that gets close to them, never again to be seen. I have this feeling in the pit of my stomach that the leaders in China go to bed at night laughing at Americans.

It is worth noting, Bob, that the TV was not invented by a radio company but by a fourteen-year-old Mormon boy, Philo Farnsworth, who in 1921 had the idea while mowing hay in rows on his father's farm. The PC was not invented by IBM, but it was Henry Roberts who developed the first commercially successful home computer, the Altair 8800. And xerography was not invented by someone in the printing business but rather by a patent attorney in New York named Chester Carlson in 1938. Truly, new ideas oftentimes come from afar and are often unencumbered by history. Don't underestimate the will and the creativity of the American people if given the space to explore. One caveat, Bob, tell NASA to keep Detroit at arm's length. Let Detroit go on doing its thing and let those who are blind to the fact that it can't be done do it.

I Think We Need to Unthink Using a Non-Zero-Sum Lens

At one point in my life, I was commuting from the East Bay (over the Bay Bridge) into San Francisco. The bridge was often a monster bottleneck. On one occasion, the traffic was backed up for several miles, and so I decided to experiment. Every time I came across a sign pointing to the Bay Bridge, I turned in the opposite direction. I wasted a lot of my time that day, but on my last wrong turn (very near the tollbooth), I was headed away from the bridge when I spotted an on-ramp that had no cars on it. I traced that on-ramp back (away from the bridge) to its entry point, and that became my new route to the bridge. What might the outcome have been if Detroit had decided to simply export cars to China? They would be more expensive that way, but then Detroit would be competing with Chinese-built cars without the benefit of all the technology Detroit had to give the Chinese in order to build their cars in China. Does Detroit have so little faith in the idea the United States can make a car that competes on quality? What if Ford had invested that $5 billion in the United States to build the perfect Chinese car? Had they done so, the money would have stayed here and the jobs would have stayed here. If you are wondering where the American middle class is, read what Forbes has to say. "The market for premium cars—anything from an Audi to the usual Italian sports cars—has increased by a compounded annual rate of 36% in the last decade, faster than the 26% annual growth in the overall Chinese passenger vehicle market during the same period. Sales of premium cars in China hit 1.25 million vehicles in 2012, making it the second biggest market in the world after the United States. The premium car market in China represented 9% of all passenger car sales in 2012, surpassing much wealthier Japan (4%) and South Korea (6%)." As Horace Mann said, "Let us not be content to wait and see what will happen, but give us the determination to make the right things happen."

EPILOGUE

Can America's Torch Be Made to Shine Once Again?

> If you do not change direction, you may end up where you are heading.
>
> —Lao Tzu

Bob, I don't want to end our conversion on a political note, but if we are to once again become the light so bright that it draws people to it, then we do need to include a discussion of leadership at the governing levels. It pains me to say that I don't see many non-zero-sum leaders in the governing (i.e., rule-making) business. To some extent, it is easy to understand because few so have any in-depth, real-world experience at leading, let alone non-zero-sum leading. Indeed, many of our governing rulers (particularly at the federal level) come from a background in trial law, which has nothing at all to do with leadership and most especially not with non-zero-sum leadership. In fact, it is the very antithesis of non-zero-sum as trial law is *all* about winning, the very definition of zero-sum leadership. Also, bear in mind that trail law is not about creating wealth (except for

131

the trail lawyers) but rather success is measured by how much wealth they effectively redistribute.

While on the subject, here is where my head is on all this. Two recent studies (one by Harvard) examined the relationship (i.e., correlation) between debt and growth. Both, independently, reached the same conclusion, although differing on the rate of decline once past the tipping point. One saw a sharp drop-off and the other a more gradual drop, but both saw a drop in growth at the point where debt exceeded 90 percent of GDP. Bob, did you know that in the four years between 2004 and 2008, the national debt rose a total of 5 percent (from 61.3 percent to 64.8 percent of GDP), while in the four years after 2008, the debt rose 46 percent from 64.8 percent to 95.2 percent and is now over 100 percent of GDP with no end in sight? In fiscal year 2013, the total interest paid on the U.S. debt was $415,688,781,248 (that's billions) at an average interest rate of 2.52 percent. Now just suppose interest rates rise to a nominal rate of 4 percent (the average rate over the past twenty years was 5.7 percent). The interest payments (at the present level of debt) would total over $680 billion. Putting that into context, that would be (in interest alone) about equal to the entire U.S. Department of Defense budget. Now fast-forward to a $20 trillion debt (projected for 2016) and a 4 percent interest rate (not at all unusual and, in fact, highly likely at that level of debt) and you get $800 billion a year in interest alone! Since we have to borrow (or print) the money to pay the interest that adds further to the debt, this is a debt that we, our children, their children, and so on ad infinitum can never hope to pay off (or even significantly reduce) and which will effectively kill off our economy. It is estimated that by 2020, over 85 percent of *all federal personal income tax* will go to pay the interest on our debt. Some nights when I go to bed, I am haunted by that prophetic pronouncement of the king of France Louis XV when he said, "Après moi, le déluge." But are we losing ground in all categories? It depends on what you see as losing ground. By at least one measure, we are making progress. In 2008, the United States was not among those listed as one of the 180 most corrupt countries in the world, but we are now listed as number

162, tied with Uruguay and far behind countries like Denmark and New Zealand. How's that for progress?

Is the situation hopeless? Challenging, to say the very least, but not yet hopeless. Bob, how about taking a flight of fantasy in one of those planes you used to fly? I think it may be helpful to get us high enough above this box so we can see beyond what is in the way and hampering our progress to rebuild our once-robust economy. A recent event may help to shed some light on the nature of the challenges that beset our efforts to create a brighter future. Watching the news a while back, Bob, I was struck by the story of a large American manufacturing firm that was planning to move its manufacturing facilities to Mexico. The governor of the state, the mayor and city manager, the unions, and others in the state that had something to offer met to put together a package of incentives to keep the plant in the United States, even offering a twenty-year no-taxes pledge and substantial concessions by the unions. The firm's response was simply that there was nothing the group could offer that compares with the hourly wages of $1.50 they would have in Mexico. This is the sort of problem the little Dutch boy can't fix by sticking his finger in the dam or by pouring billions into clean energy. Trying to create new manufacturing jobs in America, while not a lost cause, will be an uphill battle unless we embrace and unleash some of those few remaining engines of growth.

But first we have to break the cycle of billions of tax dollars going into lost causes like manufacturing solar energy cells and wind generators, which, over the long run, create very few full-time jobs. Even China can't make solar work. After years of overbuilding, China's top ten solar manufacturers have $28.8 billion of liabilities as of their latest filings; most of it is owed to government-supported institutions, according to BNEF. The shakeout has touched every one of the manufacturers. Even LDK shrinks from its height in 2011 when Xinyu-based LDK had thirty thousand employees churning out silicon wafers and solar panels. It now has about ten thousand workers, $2.8 billion in debt, and ended the second quarter of 2013 with $85 million in cash, the lowest level of cash since 2009. Its shares are 98 percent lower than their peak in September 2007. The

Chinese have come to the realization that supporting them through government-sponsored manufacturing loans isn't really working. Do we honestly think we can (or want to) compete with that? As for wind farms, they will not move the energy needle, and as far as jobs are concerned, most wind-driven generators are made in China.

Moreover, Bob, did you know that using the current efficiency numbers, generating one MW of output power using solar cells (enough to power roughly two hundred homes but no businesses) to light all the homes in the city where you and I live would require some 45,117 acres. Not a lot, I suppose, considering we have 1,014,720 acres in our county. However, since the federal government owns 86 percent of all the land in Nevada, that doesn't leave us much spare room to put our solar cells. Of course, that does nothing for the energy needs of the businesses. Imagine the solar field needed to light up Las Vegas. But let us just focus on the needs of our city. I suppose our neighboring cities and the rest of the county could use candles. Seems to me, Bob, that while trying to create *new* manufacturing jobs in America, the only thing we have come up with is attempting to generate high-paying, so-called sustainable jobs in the renewable clean energy sector. We need to be realistic; as long as wages in China are one-tenth those of the United States, we will continue to rack up failures like Solyndra, with its $535 million tax payer grant, and companies like Abound Solar with $400 million, Range Fuels with $156 million, A123 with $132 million, Ever1 with $118.5 million, Evergreen Solar with $50 million, Beacon Power with $43 million, and the list goes on and on. These were represented as America's future in geothermal, solar, even lightbulbs, and we were told "the true engine of economic growth will *always be* companies like Solyndra." All those above and more have filed for bankruptcy, and with them went all those high-paying middle-class jobs they were going to create. It is time to get real and deal with what is possible. I am not suggesting that clean energy is undesirable, but it may take a decade or more before it becomes economically practical. What, for example, if we had given NASA that same $1.4 billion to solve the problem of neutralizing or eliminating the CO_2 produced by burning coal? To start with, the EPA would not be able to make any argument for closing down coal-fired energy plants. Talk about a perfect example of zero-sum leadership; that decision would leave tens of thousands of bodies lying around where solving the "problem" will put thousands out of work in the coal-mining business and the companies that manufacture the equipment to support that effort; thousands more by the small businesses that depend on those miners, and the small towns that are home to thousands of men, women, and children, eliminating the taxes those companies and their employees pay to support the schools, police, firemen, and thousands more that operate and supply support to the coal-fired furnaces. It seems easier to take an action that requires a mere stroke of the pen than to undertake the hard work of eliminating the cause (a non-zero-sum approach), and you don't have to stare into the faces of all those affected by your action or lose so much as a minute's sleep over it. But if it is an alternative you want, how about giving the top five chemical research universities and the top five engineering universities each $100 million to work on the problem? Then pick the best (in terms of environmental impact and cost-effectiveness) solutions from among those ten and award the best chemical and the best engineered solutions to the problem with another $250 million to further study and refine their solutions. After all CO_2 is the culprit not coal.

I think if we can get past the "save the spotted owl" syndrome, we may still have a chance. This is a struggle to save (or create) the jobs of, by, and for millions of Americans. This is a fight to restore the American middle class. Unless we change our approach, and soon, all this talk about training for the jobs of the future will boil down to nothing more than how to make hotel beds more efficiently and how to flip hamburgers faster.

There has been a lot of talk about a balanced approach lately. If a balanced approached is such a good idea for taxes and spending, why not for jobs and the environment? Yes, there have been small victories here and there, but not anywhere near enough to stop the continuous and rapid implosion of our middle class. Our answer seems to be focusing on reducing the spread between incomes in search of equality rather than how to raise incomes by creating those very jobs that will lift all the ships. If we take anything from Dr. Daniel Bell's 1976 book, he correctly foresaw the essential liabilities of the postindustrial capitalist society, such as the diffusion of global capital, the imbalance of international trade, and the decline of the manufacturing sector in the United States. The time has come for us to man up. Our culture has a number of unique characteristics. Among those is an entrepreneurial quality that, given the room (and incentives) to grow, is capable of creating tens of thousands (if not millions) of jobs. We are among the most creative countries in the world, and creativity has been an engine of job creation for over 150 years. But we need incentives to unleash this creative and innovative spirit, and I don't mean government subsidies to compete with China on solar cells, a losing proposition from the start.

But, Bob, it will take a bunch of non-zero-sum leaders to make it happen or, I should say, *let* it happen in order to do what might help us rebuild a sustainable (and prosperous) middle class. I do believe it is still possible to create more old-line manufacturing jobs. If we climb back in that plane of yours and look around, what we see is that most large manufacturing (and service) companies are offshoring— with a vengeance. There is no stopping them if they are to survive in a global economy. But what's this I see, Bob? It seems a lot of smaller companies are managing to compete, in part because they have to and in part because they are too small to leverage (or otherwise) take advantage of any potential added savings by offshoring and just small enough to avoid (so far) becoming the targets of hungry global competitors. *These* are the job-creating companies we need to support. Creating tax breaks for companies like Apple and GE will do nothing to hold back the tide. Clearly, with all the smarts we have, we can come up with a plan for creating the space these companies need to grow; they are a significant part of our future. Here is where we need to be (moderately?) creative and take less in corporate income taxes in trade for the income taxes paid by employed individuals and from FICA and SDI taxes. Now add to that the savings on unemployment and food stamps (which in our state amounts to over $750 a month for two people). So what would it take? To start with, any change in small business taxes should *not* be based on hiring more employees. If you have a thriving business *and* you have relief from corporate income taxes during your growth years, you will find the means to add more employees when you have a need for them. If you don't have the customers, even a $10,000 credit is not enough to offset the cost of hiring someone you have no need for. Remember, what we are trying to accomplish is to create jobs, not reduce profits, and the best way to do that is not government incentives but for the government to provide an environment that enables and encourages economic growth. Perhaps a 0 percent corporate tax rate for those with fewer than ten or even fifteen employees. At these early stages, profits are the vital seeds of growth. Once given the resources needed to grow the business enough to get to a sustainable level of employees, we might then charge a maximum of 10 percent flat corporate tax up to twenty-five or even fifty employees and 15 percent maximum until they exceed one hundred employees. There will be those that argue this creates a disincentive to hire the 101st employee. I don't know of any entrepreneur who, having a growing business, would decide to stop at this point of success in growing his or her business because it may cost them more in taxes. Now exempt all those companies with fewer than one hundred employees, give them all a waiver from the Affordable Care Act, and in all ways possible, significantly reduce the burden of excessive government regulations, without sacrificing the workers' or the public's health or safety, and such changes may just make the difference. We need to stop playing politics with companies like Boeing when they want to move more of their production to South Carolina. We should stand up and applaud them, for the other option is moving that production to China, which they have so far resisted. I say good for them! They deserve a corporate medal of honor for being a good citizen, but instead they get harassment from the NLRB. But a recent update: Boeing Co. is exploring whether to open a factory in China to complete work on its top-selling 737-model jetliners.

So is there a needle in our haystack? I think so, but it is being treated like it has points at both ends. What is it that can kill four birds (should someone want to do that) with one stone or, better still, hit a grand slam home run at the bottom of the ninth when you are behind by three runs? It seems every time the subject of energy comes up, it is treated like a four-letter word. We need to create hundreds of thousands of good-paying jobs, and energy may be our *best* option to produce (manufacture) that cannot be offshored or outsourced. One cannot outsource the generation of nuclear power or undertake hydraulic fracturing or drill for oil *in* America *from* China or Mexico. If it could be done, they would be doing it. You can't mine coal from across the pacific, and remember, it is not coal that is bad but carbon dioxide, so we need to spend our money solving that problem instead of trying to compete with China in making solar cells. Within ten years, America could be approaching energy independence (or at the very least, importing only from those countries that actually like us), creating millions of new jobs in energy and its spin-offs, contributing billions in new taxes, shutting off funds to those countries using their oil proceeds to support terrorists or build nuclear bombs, and at the same time, driving down fuel costs, which, of course, makes America more competitive. So the very first thing we need to do is to open the energy spigot, wide open, and that includes pipelines from Canada to Texas. We are not at the point where the only (best?) option is sustainable solar or wind power, but perhaps with another ten or twenty years to develop cost-effective technology, we can ease into these other power sources instead of trying to jump-start them with billions of taxpayer's dollars.

Bob, when you look deep into this, you will find some very strange (read: bizarre) things going on. For example, did you know that our government forced one of our American oil producers to stop drilling off the coast of Alaska because a village of 250 people seventy miles away *may* be harmed by emissions? Our approach seems to be to create jobs by taking all our energy resources off our table. This is like trying to win at Monopoly without owning Boardwalk and Park

Place. For example, Cuba announced that it would begin drilling in the Gulf of Mexico by the end of 2013. There is no doubt that drilling will soon be done off America's coast, but sadly not by us. Thanks to a treaty signed by President Carter, the new oil and gas resources that will be discovered in that region will be discovered by Russia and Cuba to their economic benefit. Normally, economic zones extend two hundred miles off a country's coastline, but in 1977, President Carter signed a treaty with Cuba that essentially split the difference and created for the communist country an "exclusive economic zone" extending from the western tip of Cuba north virtually to Key West. Cuba has divided its side of the Florida Straits into fifty-nine parcels and put them up for lease. Foreign countries, including China and India, have acquired the rights to develop sixteen of them. "This is the irony of ironies," complained Charles Drevna, executive vice president of the National Petrochemical & Refiners Association. "We have chosen to lock up our resources and stand by to be spectators while these two come in and benefit from things right in our own backyard." This allows Russia's Zarubezhneft oil concern to work with the Cubanpetroleo monopoly to explore and develop the oil riches of the North Cuban Basin off Florida. Why is it that Russia, Cuba, and others can drill off the coast of Florida but we can't? The U.S. Geological Survey recently estimated the North Cuban Basin contains as much as nine billion barrels of oil and twenty-two trillion cubic feet of natural gas.

We need to apply some non-zero-sum thinking to our present and future strategy for creating good-paying sustainable jobs. Trying to repatriate jobs when, with the highest corporate tax rates in the world, an antibusiness political climate, and wage rates in China as low as 10 percent of those in America, it is like trying to push a string uphill. Bob, did you know that if the rate of labor participation was the same as it was in 2008, the unemployment rate would not be 5 percent to 6 percent but over 11 percent. The number of people unable to find work and no longer counted as looking (and therefore not counted as unemployed) is the reason we *seem* to be making progress. Of course, it also helps bring the unemployment rate down when you factor in that between 2008 and mid-2012, the number of federal employees has grown by 11.4 percent.

Yes, focusing on things like infrastructure may be another way to create some jobs, but to make the argument that it would lower the unemployment rate in the construction industry shows how naive many politicians are. The building or repairing of roads and bridges will not move the needle with regard to carpenters, electricians, roofers, drywall installers, and virtually all those engaged in the construction industry. I do think we need to focus some resources on the infrastructure, but I don't see why the federal government should be spending Nevada's money to repair a bridge in Minnesota or why Minnesota should help pay for a highway in Nevada. Federal funds should be used only in situations where federal works (e.g., federal highways) are involved or where there has been catastrophic damage due to a natural disaster. Yes, the federal government should *lend* the money to New Jersey to repair the damage from the Boardwalk fire, but why should taxpayers from Tennessee pay for that? Natural disasters like Sandy and Katrina are appropriate situations where federal aid is essential to rebuilding the damage and the lives of those affected. But I see no reason for Georgia to help pay for repairing roads in Massachusetts. It is up to the states to maintain the infrastructure of their own state. Why should states that do this finance states that don't?

So let's really focus more on things like creating real jobs and opportunity for individual growth (and earnings) instead of income and social equality. Let's get on with rebuilding the American dream, which has nothing to do with income redistribution but is (and always has been) all about building ladders on which people can climb. It's time to lay down our shovels and pick up hammers and get to work. The end result is the possibility of reducing our debt (assuming unlikely prudent spending by our lawmakers), creating millions of new middle-class jobs, the return of a sound housing market and all that goes with that, restoring the dollar as the world's currency, and building a solid foundation on which to construct a future for generations to come.

All those in favor, raise your hand. Wow, this is awesome, Bob; almost every person raised their hand.

CPSIA information can be obtained at www.ICGtesting.com
Printed in the USA
BVOW02*1120310316

442363BV00001B/2/P